BE
GOOD
WITH
MONEY

MICHELLE ARPIN BEGINA

Contents

1. Financial Plot Twist   1
2. Secrecy Bias   11
3. Financial Self-Sabotage & the Four Emotional Money Drivers   27
4. Your Moneyhood   39
5. Money Scripts   51
6. Your Moneyself   67
7. The Duality of Money—How to Allow What We Want   79
8. Command Your New Money Relationship   91
9. Self-Talk—The Invisible Force   109
10. Connect the Dots to Your New Moneyself   123
11. Write the Eulogy   135
12. Talk it Out: Validation, Information, & Advice   145
13. Abracadabra!   157

Bibliography   167
Take It to The Bank (Acknowledgments)   173
About the Author   177

For Alex and Nick

Financial Plot Twist

*L*et me start by saying I was crazy about my parents.

Growing up, I saw my Mom and Dad at their highest and best: living the American dream, building a business from the ground up, and capable of doing anything they could think of. They were energetic, fun, and downright charming, always gathering large groups of friends for epic parties.

In the early days of their household moving and storage business, money was tight. Simply paying the rent, keeping food on the table, and making payments on the moving truck that was our sole source of income was a struggle. My father performed the work of a five-man crew all by himself for the first few years and fell into bed exhausted—only to get up and do it all again the next day.

To make ends meet, my mom clipped coupons and traded S&H green stamps from the supermarket for necessities. My brother and I wore winter coats that were three sizes too large to avoid replacing them each year. Despite how tight money was, we had what we needed, and we had each other. I always felt safe.

I loved having conversations with my father about business. He taught me about portfolios, taxes and interest rates, and the inner workings of how his company ran. He showed me how he tracked his sales "closing ratios," calculated moving estimates, and details about how he managed his crew.

He talked about ethics and making hard choices. He had the epitome of a growth mindset. He followed his own passions, learned to fly, built cars from scratch, got into photography (he got me into it), competed with my mom as an amateur ballroom dancer. I ate that stuff up.

Mom was a fashionista. She taught me how to sew, how to dress, and that it's never too late to pursue a dream. My mother was introspective and deep and one of the most empathetic people I knew. She was also an incredible jazz dancer.

Within a few years of being in business, my parents secured government work doing military moves, which paid well. However, the downside was that government payments came in big lump sums, and often this would mean months of no income. Managing this well required planning and budgeting, which was most definitely *not* my parents' strong suit.

Our erratic income aside, we moved into a home, and my brother and I went to good schools. We started talking about me going to college, and although my Dad would joke about my M-R-S degree, in truth, they were very encouraging.

I was always a nerd. I loved school and school loved me. Learning was my jam. It simply lit me up and everyone could tell. Mom was tickled by the idea that I'd be the first in the family to go to college. I remember discussing it with her in middle school, and we were united in our goal: getting me into a good college.

By the end of eighth grade, my mom had convinced my father to pay tuition for me to attend a higher-performing high school. Once there, we did everything from extra reading retention classes to SAT tutoring to help me prepare. I was excited, and so were my parents. They bragged about my plans with family and friends.

In the summer between junior and senior year, my father and I took legendary father-daughter tours of college campuses. These were good times: long car rides, singing Billy Joel songs together on the radio, and talking about big dreams.

College was an investment, and I was nervous because money had a tendency to blow up. Even though we all struggled with the financial famine in between big government checks, it seemed like Dad wrestled with it the most. His way of coping was to buy himself a hard-earned toy when they hit paydirt. And by toy, I mean a sports car or a private airplane or a boondoggle in Atlantic City. Unfortunately, those treats often came at the expense of food security, taxes, mortgage payments, and savings. But in this case, he managed to put the tuition funds in reserve—my father showed me the passbook savings account with the entire amount for school. As a family, we were in sync mentally, emotionally, and financially—we were ready. I couldn't wait to soak up life as a fine arts major at UC and paint and draw my way through life.

And Then...

One Saturday morning, the summer before college was to start, my father invited me to our slip at the marina to see our new yacht. Before leaving the house, I saw what I hoped to be a college acceptance letter. Excitedly, I brought it with me to open with Dad.

When I showed my father, he gave me a sheepish grin. Then, with an "aw shucks" shrug of his shoulders, he said, "We can't afford to send you to school anymore."

What?

Wait.

What?!

On a whim, my parents had bought this yacht with my college fund.

That's right. My. Parents. Blew. My college fund. On. A. Yacht.

Painted on the side was its name—*Another Toy*.

I was gobsmacked.

As I stood there, the dock and the boats around me blurred, and reality drifted out of reach. In my disbelief, my childhood flashed before me. This was shocking, but not out of character. Somehow, it added up.

Hope, certainty, optimism drained from my body.

The dreams of friends I'd make and stuff I'd learn— was now a memory. So was my family's shared goal. And my trust.

I was alone.

What I Learned

A financial plot twist can be unsettling—throwing us for a loop. When this happens, we tend to linger in a state of disbelief or denial, and focus on one thing: survival. I know I did.

My parents not only pulled the financial rug out from under me, but they also shook my self-worth and sense of what it meant to belong to a family.

Unable to process my heartbreak, and with no tools to

guide me, I stayed in a state of denial and I did the only thing I could do. I pulled myself up by the bootstraps, used my parents for housing and food, got a hodgepodge of jobs, and worked my tail off.

Don't get me wrong, though. The stench of that betrayal clouded every thought and interaction with my parents from that point forward. I was judgmental, edgy, and impatient with them. Nothing they said or did was good or good enough. While I'd always trusted they did their best—not any more. They suddenly could do no right.

It felt terrible. Looking back, I now know I was repressing my feelings. And the fact that they never brought it up to talk about (either) made it even worse. I think my mother avoided the conversation with me because she was ashamed of what she'd done and was unable to face the pain of having hurt me. My father, well, I'm not so sure he thought so deeply about any of this.

So that's where I came from, but it's not where I stayed.

Where I Went

My "sudden financial independence" sparked an obsession with money—a la Scarlett O'Hara, "I'll never be hungry again!" My insatiable curiosity about managing money helped me focus away from my family and my painful experience. Instead, I fixated on mastering the psychology of finance, switched my major, and got all kinds of alphabet to show I did it: my AD, BS, CFP®, CIMA®.

I started with an associate's degree at a local community college (big fan of community colleges), and within ten years, I had earned my bachelor's degree at Rider University. Later, I would also earn a graduate certificate at Kansas State University in financial therapy.

That's a fancy way of saying I solved the mystery of my parent's dock crime by studying what drives our financial beliefs and behaviors. I see the same concepts echoed from my parents, clients, friends, and even myself. I also see the potential in all of us to identify and change those things —if we want to. It's not as hard as one may think.

The Poverty of Prosperity and What I Want to Share with You

I've been on a mission my whole adult life to leverage what I've learned about the psychology of finance to help people up-level the trajectory of their money story across the board, and reach their full financial potential.

My parents were not alone in their financial struggles, and my experiencing a financial plot twist is not unique. Many people, including many of the clients I've worked with, share the same challenge. It's more common than you may think.

"Poverty of prosperity" is a term for when we make a lot of money but keep little of it. Simply put, it means being financially and emotionally bankrupt. Big-picture, it refers to situations where there is a lack of wealth and resources despite the presence of economic growth and opportunity. The poverty of prosperity is when people don't benefit from the resources and opportunities that they have. On a personal level, it's spending more than what is coming in. It's over-committing financially. It's when your eyes are bigger than your wallet. Sound familiar?

If we make so much, or even enough, why can't we hold on to it? Or at least spend wisely? Grow our wealth? We can. But often, it takes a little awareness, will, and a little effort. Our money stories and hidden distortions compel us to act against our own best interests. This happens for a multitude of reasons: secrecy bias, financial self-sabotage, moneyhood, moneyself, and money scripts, or lack of priorities or plans.

Once we understand ourselves better, we can do better. And the good news is: it's totally changeable. You can make your money, keep some, spend some, and experience the full range of freedom, security, and abundance that money provides.

Since 2000, I've talked with thousands of people about their finances. I served as vice president at Merrill Lynch and Morgan Stanley and I'm currently a managing partner and financial advisor at Snowden Lane Partners.

I have successfully lobbied for financial psychology education in New Jersey schools. I helped rewrite *National Standards for Financial Literacy* in partnership with the American Public Education Foundation (APEF).

Once I better understood my own relationship with money, everything changed for me. Everything.

Here's the deal. There isn't one magical formula to liberate yourself from the secrecy and shame that most people have around money. There's not. But, I have narrowed it down to six transformational concepts for people who want to be as good with money as they are in the rest of their lives.

These are the most in-depth set of money therapy exercises you can find anywhere.

We can choose to up-level our money story whenever we want to. Once our true money story is made visible to us, we can begin to shift our money reality and reach our full financial potential. The book's two phases will guide you. First, chapters 1 through 6 talk about where your money story comes from, and how childhood experiences can create secrecy and shame. Next, chapters 7 through 12 will show you how to change your financial reality, by talking about money in deeper and more meaningful ways.

Secrecy and shame evolve into untrue stories that set up shop in our subconscious. It's these kinds of secrets—which sometimes we don't even realize we have—that keep us from talking about money at all, and stop us from reaching our full financial potential.

Once you understand your relationship with money, and learn to talk about it, everything changes. You deserve to have and feel abundance from the money you bring in. I want to help you do that.

Finding my voice changed my financial future by liberating me from the shame and betrayal of secrecy. I know that helping you find your voice and tell your money story will liberate you and up-level your financial future, too.

I share my personal story for a number of reasons. First and foremost, it's to help others understand and escape out of a toxic relationship with money. If you have ever felt or now feel hopeless, insignificant, discouraged, anxious, confused, inadequate, uncertain, alone, lost and/or ashamed, you are not alone. Far from it. I, for one, am with you.

If you have more debt or less savings than you think you "should," if you don't feel like you have strong success guardrails, if you are winging it and know that something is holding you back, but aren't sure what that is, I get it.

If you make enough money, but you don't *feel* like you have enough—or if you're not experiencing the wealth or abundance you're bringing in, I get it. I want to help you reach your full financial potential.

The cure to feeling bad about money, or like there isn't enough, is choice. That's right—choice is the solution, and I will show you how to cultivate financial choices in your life. I will show you how to analyze your influences, assess what's working, grow your self-knowledge, and develop a mindset of choice.

Our real challenge in our relationship with money isn't juggling work and school, or even finances. It's ruminating in isolation on the shock and shame of our financial stories or choices.

Be Good with Money will teach you to recognize the limitations in the old way of thinking about money and give you the prompts you need to see new possibilities for your life. After reading it, you will know what drives your beliefs, whether those beliefs serve you, and how to change them if they don't. You will know who to ask for help and what to say. Rather than being stressed about finances, you will feel a sense of ease, and—might I suggest—perhaps some badassery, too. Who doesn't want to feel like a badass about money?

Bottom line: we need to shift the conversation about money. Identifying and understanding our beliefs is only the first step. Talking about money differently than we ever have before is what changes our lives. We need to start talking about the emotions behind our money so that we can transform our relationship with money from toxic to talking it out. A toxic relationship is where we are silent about our beliefs, attitudes, and behaviors; confuse money with self-worth; avoid the topic; and focus too much on earning as a way to solve all of life's problems.

You have to show up for yourself as part therapy patient, part CSI analyst. You have to be willing to answer questions, hand-write notes, and connect the dots.

To accomplish this at the highest level, I invite you to leverage journaling and—in some cases—talking it out. Why journaling? As Allison Fallon explains in *The Power of Writing It Down*, "Sometimes memories are buried in our subconscious. We don't often find what's in our subconscious until we write about it. We don't see the connections that set us free until we find the time to write them down. Writing can heal your life from the inside out—body, mind, and soul."

If that doesn't convince you to grab your journal, consider this other gem from Fallon, "Writing hands you back the keys to your own life."

Grab your journal and a pen, friend. We're getting your keys to the castle—stat.

A healthy money relationship is where we know we can talk about it any time, we know what we can and cannot afford, our values align with our wallets, and we are comfortable with our status. Talking about our money in this open way—exploring beliefs, feelings, and actions—is how we blast through shame and secrecy. When you do this, the whole trajectory of your life will change because you will be good with money and money will be good with you. *Be Good with Money* is where that shift begins.

2

Secrecy Bias

*M*oney is something we play hide and seek from—with ourselves and each other. Why? Because we've learned it's taboo through inherited beliefs and behaviors of secrecy and shame. Centuries ago, privacy was held as an aristocratic virtue, along with independence and stoicism. However, these values and their outcomes shifted greatly with the information era, and some simply did not age well.

We all do the same four things with money: earn, spend, save, and give. Universally, across all cultures, and in all periods of time. And all four of those things are shrouded in secrecy: secrets between our family and loved ones, secrets between co-workers and business partners, secrets from and within ourselves. That secrecy and silence is the number one thing keeping us from realizing our full financial potential.

Am I a Jerkhole If I Talk About Money?

The first line of my TEDx Talk drew nervous laughter, and I don't blame the audience. After all, the question, "How much credit card debt do you have?" tends to stop people in their tracks, wide-eyed and uncertain. The laughter that came from the audience was the kind that pours out of us all at those most inappropriate times—while attending a funeral, being fired from a job, or during a particularly poignant moment at church.

You know, *those* kinds of moments. When we mask uncomfortable feelings with a "happy-cry;" laughing on the outside while crying on the inside.

The thing is, almost no one asks us direct, personal money questions. How many times have you asked someone what their net worth is? How much money they have in their retirement account? How often have you been asked how much money you make? Most people default to the belief that talking about money is forbidden, and we either wait for the "right time" to talk about it, or we avoid the topic entirely.

In a recent survey, 70% of Americans think it's rude to talk about money. Even among people who have financial advisors, 64% don't feel like they have anyone to talk with about their finances. My own friends tell me that they "wouldn't dream about talking with their advisor about their money problems." What? Isn't that their job? I know it's mine!

Early in my career, I was surprised by how many of my successful, high-income, professional clients resisted real money conversations. Over time however, I realized that when someone who likes to be considered a universally high performer struggles with an important part of their life, like money, they are prone to hiding it. The worry seems to be, "If someone learns I struggle with something as important as money, they'll think I'm a fraud or will begin to doubt my abilities elsewhere." The adage "How we do one thing is how we do everything" is a dangerous belief when we're working to improve our financial health.

My contention is, "How we do one thing is *not* how we do everything."

We can both diet and binge eat, go to church and cheat on our spouse, save in our retirement accounts and charge more than we can afford on our credit cards.

We often act as if our abilities are domain-specific. They are most certainly not. We can absolutely learn to consciously transfer the strengths that we've developed elsewhere into our financial lives.

So no—emphatically no—you are not a jerkhole if you talk about money. In fact, it's the contrary. Talking about money is an astute, productive step to take if you want to reach your full financial potential, and I will show you how.

The Persistent Resistance of Secrecy Bias

The concept of silence and secrecy was planted early in my upbringing.

With no intervention, it carried on for decades.

As a teenager at our marina, sometime between hearing my father's words, "We can't afford to send you to school," and leaving the dock, I decided never to speak of that moment again—not inside or outside of my house for more than 30 years. And from that day forward, shame had me under its thumb, a hostage to secrecy.

And I buried that secret deep, so that the pain of betrayal wouldn't eat me alive.

I call this persistent resistance to talking about money the Secrecy Bias. A bias is a psychological distortion that operates like a funhouse mirror where parts of the reflection are unnaturally skinny or weirdly inflated. We see something that resembles the truth, but is systemically and pervasively distorted.

A bias can create the psychological wiggle-room that we need to justify a decision that isn't financially sound—like a blue Jaguar instead of health insurance or a yacht instead of a college education. When we hide our financial decisions and gloss over their implications in conversation, we are immersed in the secrecy bias. This limits our ability to create new, healthier money habits through our unwillingness to talk about it.

Secrecy bias is a tendency or cultural norm where we are taught or learn to be quiet and secretive about financial matters, including income, wealth, debts, and spending habits. This bias is often rooted in social, cultural, or familial beliefs and practices that view discussions about money as taboo, impolite, or inappropriate. Secrecy bias can lead to a lack of financial literacy, difficulties in financial planning, and challenges in addressing economic disparities, as it hinders open and honest discussions about money, its management, and its impact on individual and societal levels. This bias may also contribute to perpetuating myths or misunderstandings about wealth and financial success, as well as exacerbating feelings of shame or inadequacy related to financial struggles or mistakes.

Secrets, Jaguars, and Real Conversations We Never Had

When I was 10, my mother took a trip to visit family for a few weeks. While she was away, my father saw a dark blue Jaguar at a client's house. He called my mom, elated. He told her that he had found his dream car at a great price, and this was his big chance.

Mom said, "No," in no uncertain terms.

She wanted to pay back taxes and health insurance premiums. He relented, and they hung up a little while later.

Not long after, he rolled up in the driveway with… wait for it: the blue Jag. He showed it off to me, with the air of a cavalier hotshot. Then he swore me to secrecy.

When Mom called to check in on us, I felt like a traitor. I kept his secret, while part of me hoped that my mom would return, put her foot down and fix things. Would this be enough to finally make some changes?

I remember wondering how he thought he'd be able to keep the car from her. Was he hoping she wouldn't notice? Please.

When she first caught sight of the car, she went completely, eerily still. Then, she simultaneously broke into tears and screamed, "When are you going to grow up?"

My father accused my mother of being hysterical and over-emotional.

While the argument started about the car, it quickly grew to verbal brawl about *everything*. The situation escalated, erupted, and left all of us drained and miserable. But, despite this argument and many others like it, nothing changed substantively in our money story.

This is because arguing about money is not the same as talking about money.

Quarreling about the consequences of our money decisions, whether that's credit card bills, late payments, or unauthorized purchases like my father's Jaguar, happens naturally. We get upset, blame each other, and before we know it, the disagreement has spiraled out of control.

Individual money issues tend to get tangled in other

unresolved money issues, resulting in comments like, "You never pay the bills on time," or, "You just don't care about our future," or, my Mom's favorite, "Are you ever going to grow up?"

Money arguments become "all or nothing" all the time —but there is a different approach.

My goal for this book is to give you another way to talk about money so that you can reach your full financial potential. First, you'll uncover your true beliefs, experiences, and feelings about money. Then, you'll learn how to have productive conversations about money with the people who matter most.

That's what my parents couldn't do. It's what I became obsessed about, and it's what I'm going to help you to do so you can avoid the kind of fallout that we experienced over and over in our family.

What Secrecy Costs

In my observation, secrecy is *the* bias that has the biggest failure rate when it comes to money. The secrecy bias acts like cloud cover, blocking the rays of the sun from shining on our skin's receptors and creating strength-building vitamin D. The ability to reason cannot develop when we're cut off from talking to others. In our silence, we become trapped with our distorted understanding, losing out on perspectives that would help us to see a bigger picture or take a longer view. Without opportunities to speak openly about money, we give away all of our powers of independence, critical thinking, control, and ultimately, choice.

Money secrets in childhood (i.e., your parents *never* talked about money in front of others or financial information was intentionally withheld from members of your family) have damaging side effects in adulthood and can lead to overspending, a perpetual lack of trust, and excessive worrying about money. Money secrets in families are especially damaging to women. When women are not raised in a home where transparency about money is valued, they are more likely to settle for lower salaries and are less confident negotiating in the workplace.

In secrecy and silence, we don't get to learn from experts or others who've had experiences similar to our own. Without an outside vantage point, we may downplay or catastrophize situations and be unable to keep ourselves from digging deeper into a hole. Secrecy bias creates a negative framing around talking about money, leading us to erroneously believe that there's more to lose than to gain by being open about our money situation. On the other hand, by sharing, reasoning, and questioning our money relationships, we learn about ourselves and others. When we share, we gain compassion, respect, perspective, and fresh ideas. These outcomes of sharing can create a sense of hope and renewed optimism, something we desperately crave when we are worried about our financial future. Empathy is often the result of a meaningful conversation, especially when the listener is committed to understanding the other person's perspective. Secrets, unwanted behaviors, and financial precarity are forms of suffering; being understood opens the door to grace—for yourself and for your journey. There's magic in being witnessed.

Whether we end up fooling ourselves into thinking that things are better than they are, or whether we become shame-filled and afraid that others will judge us harshly if they know our truth, we are missing the very available opportunity to improve our situation and build financial stability. It simply takes an outside perspective and accountability to change our financial situation. Both of these require us to discuss our financial situation and habits openly with others.

The burden of carrying secrets extends beyond mental stress and loneliness to unstable finances, avoidable losses, legal and tax issues—even regret. Withholding financial information erodes trust in both personal and professional relationships, and are contributing factors in outcomes like divorce, job denial, and employment termination.

The stakes of keeping financial secrets and an inability to cope with financial problems could not be higher, *as the ultimate price can be the loss of life itself.*

According to the World Health Organization, "Many suicides happen impulsively in moments of crisis with a breakdown in the ability to deal with life stresses, such as financial problems, relationship break-up, or chronic pain and illness." A 2021 Pew Research Center report highlights that concerns over financial security and personal health are closely linked to heightened psychological distress, potentially leading to severe outcomes like suicidal thoughts or actions.

The combination of secrecy, isolation, and lack of support may create a perilous cycle that magnifies the psychological toll of financial burdens. Meanwhile, open communication and robust support systems mitigate financial stress.

Our Financial Systems Don't Help

When it comes to transparency and truth, our established systems are not supportive of frank conversations about our money. According to the Financial Industry Regulatory Authority (FINRA), our obligation as financial advisors is to discern "essential information" which are those required to "ensure that the essential facts concerning your customer are accurate and updated." While I believe that knowing my client's relationship and habits with money are essential facts, this is not the usual interpretation of these regulations.

As part of their role, financial advisors are obligated to ensure that their client is who they say they are, and that their assets are reported accurately. While this restricted job description doesn't necessarily create secrecy—nothing is stopping me from supporting my clients in a deeper way —it also doesn't facilitate an open and honest discussion of someone's financial upbringing, nor does it lead to under- standing of their money preferences or behavioral habits. Essentially, financial systems were established to comply with rules, regulations, and laws—not factor in emotions. The system is very responsive to the special handling instructions of accounts, but not at all responsive to the human factor including hopes, aspirations, fears, and other feelings. This impediment to open and honest communication makes it difficult for people to get the advice and support they need.

Even in *my* practice, where nothing about the feelings about money is off-limits to talk about, there are occasional client "confessions" that come after months, or even years, of working together when he or she finally admits to important information they've withheld.

Andrew

One example of this was with my client, Andrew. Andrew was raised by his grandparents, and most of his ideas about being good with money came from emulating them. As a child, he'd sit in a club chair in his grandfather's study, warmed by a crackling fire, reviewing stock prices in the newspaper, and tracking them on a large portfolio ledger. Andrew lovingly recalls an old world, English aristocrat, smoking jacket vibe as he learned about earnings and savings, the compound effects of investing, and not being too showy with what you have. His grandparents were from the greatest generation, and excellent mentors of fiscal responsibility, prudence, and self-control.

Upon their passing, Andrew inherited a life-changing amount of money. He cherishes the fact that the two most significant people in his life entrusted him with such a substantial amount of money, but struggled to feel worthy of receiving this windfall. For a long time, he internalized the pressure while doing his best to measure up to their belief in his ability to manage and preserve it. He felt like the inheritance was "their" money, not his.

Andrew continued to live on the shoestring he was used to living on. He agonized over every financial detail and kept tight control of his spending, limiting himself to only bare necessities. No one in real life, including me, told him to live like that. He conducted himself in a way that mirrored his perception of his grandparents' expectations. And that worked for Andrew for the first 18 months.

Then suddenly, the pendulum swung in the other direction. Andrew rebelled, said yes to virtually everything his family wanted, and began spending six times his monthly budget. In advance of receiving the second and final installment of the inheritance, he knew he needed to be more responsible.

At my request and after a lot of initial resistance, we were able to take an honest look at his expenses. The news was sobering. At his current rate of spending, we confirmed that his money would run out before his daughter reached middle school. So, we recalibrated. We spent weeks pouring over Excel spreadsheets detailing every penny he'd spent. Together, we created a new spending plan, and he agreed to a monthly account withdrawal to meet expenses while leaving the remaining investment portfolio alone to grow future security.

A few weeks into his new plan, Andrew came back to my office and shared that he was spending much more money each month than he had disclosed. He was regularly running up his credit cards to high balances and then taking large chunks of money out of his inheritance to pay them off. The withdrawals were large enough—$30k a month—to render our financial plan moot. Everything needed to be redone.

He apologized repeatedly for wasting my time, taking the complete blame, and speaking of himself in the harshest terms. It was painful to hear him attack his own character when he told me about his omission. It was only after the burden of his secret became too much—when he simply had to face his perceived risk that I might be too angry or frustrated to continue working with him—that he opened up and told me the truth. Opening up to me about his true debt took a lot of courage, especially since he judged himself so harshly.

What a lonely place for him to have been—alone with his thoughts, void of empathy or perspective. Feeling isolated with your money troubles is not healthy. First of all, it feels terrible. Without a sounding board, it's very common to sink into feelings of shame, guilt, dread, and doom. When these feelings go unchallenged, they run rampant, unchecked, until things feel so desperate that we are finally willing to ask for help. This usually happens after our financial situation has taken a hit, and there's an even bigger mess to clean up.

Financial Self-Sabotage

Like many people, Andrew's silence, secrecy, and shame could've bankrupted and ruined him financially. For many people, it does.

At the root of any financial problem is a sneaky suspect: secrecy. Secrecy is one of the most direct paths to unbalancing our emotional drivers, which leads to financial self-sabotage in all its forms.

When we struggle with money, we can catastrophize a spillover failure effect, which can in turn tighten the vice grip of secrecy, and cause a spiral. I'm a staunch proponent of the idea that "How you do one thing *is not* how you do everything."

However, what I see too often is that people don't pause long enough to realize, "I'm a success at large, but I struggle in this one area—money." If you are successful in other parts of your life, you can be successful with money, too. Overcoming financial self-sabotage takes some understanding and grace.

My dear, late friend and psychologist Howard Farkas captured Andrew's dilemma—that financial self-sabotage is conflicting values and competing commitments based on the duality of the human need to belong and the human need for autonomy. In other words, if I do too much of my own thing by spending freely on the things that I want, then relationships suffer. On the other hand, if I go along with what others need/want by putting the financial needs of others ahead of my own, then I lose myself. Too much freedom can lead to isolation because we alienate others. Too much belonging can lead to over-prioritizing others and self-sacrificing.

In the context of the four main emotional drivers of our money decisions (security, power, freedom, love), it's the inability to resolve this conflict that leads to financial self-sabotage. The real risk happens when we've not questioned or challenged our beliefs, and therefore, we've made a subconscious or even unconscious decision for ourselves. The danger is in internalizing someone else's external beliefs or expectations of us about our need to belong versus our need for autonomy.

Financial self-sabotage can detonate when there is a lack of self-knowledge and awareness. This is correctable by increasing your awareness of your financial flashpoints, moneyisms, moneyself, and money scripts and working though the journal prompts in the next few chapters.

Secrecy Bias Exercises

Please journal about how secrecy bias impacts your present-day financial decisions, factoring in timeframes, priorities, and self-sabotage. Take your time. Careful thought here will pay off many times.

1. **From Childhood:** List any general or specific instances when grown-ups, in hushed tones or with dramatic flair, told you to zip it about the family finances. What types of behind-closed-doors behavior did you witness, such as fumbling through secret envelopes of cash in the dead of night? On a scale of 1-5, 5 being fully transparent, how openly did your family discuss money matters? On a scale of 1-5, 5 being excellent, what kind of money example did your primary caregivers set? In what ways did these early experiences influence your current approach to money and financial discussions?

2. **Present Day—Secrecy Bias:** In what situations do you find yourself uncomfortable or even squirming when the conversation veers toward money? Perhaps it's fees, salary, savings, taxes, home ownership, or debt. On a scale of 1-5—5 being fully transparent and an open book, 1 being like a vault, guarding your financial status like a state secret—how open are you about your money? How does secrecy or transparency impact the quality of your relationship with your finances? Your relationship with others? How might secrecy be shaping your financial choices?

3. **Present Day—Financial Self-Sabotage:** Are there times when you prioritize the need for connection and belonging over your own financial freedom and autonomy? Or vice versa? How does this affect your financial well-being and overall life satisfaction? In what ways does it help you and in what ways does it hurt you?

4. **Unmasking Your Financial Nemesis:** Reflect on your financial self-sabotage tendencies. Identify three recurring patterns in your financial behavior that work against you. Can you identify how secrecy bias contributes to these actions?

5. **Big Picture:** What is secrecy bias costing you?

3

Financial Self-Sabotage & the Four Emotional Money Drivers

*C*oco Chanel said, "The best things in life are free. The second best things are very, very expensive." Money can buy a lot of things that are fun to wear, fun to drive, and fun to have. And the four most influential motivations behind why and how we use our money for ourselves and others—security, power, freedom, and love—are not packaged and available for purchase on Amazon. There are no problems with any of these feelings or drivers —unless or until the motivation gets out of balance. When the motivation gets out of balance, from chasing the feelings that money cannot buy, devastating problems can arise out of seemingly nowhere. At that point, when we have an overemphasis on or an imbalance of these emotions, they become very expensive. And when we chase a feeling money cannot buy, it's time to sound the alarm.

Financially, people manage their money (or don't) based on the big four. Each has an upside and a downside, and the conflict between the two sides creates financial self-sabotage. These drivers operate like love languages for many people. In other words, they are the motivations behind why we do what we do with money—these motivations are behind why we earn, spend, save, and/or give away the money we do. These drivers are the influence behind every financial decision we make, and can override rational thought.

Security, power, freedom, and love, as motivations, are not rigidly separated or isolated; they can blend in diverse mixtures and intensities, forming a broad emotional spectrum. This means we have the ability to embrace several of these emotions simultaneously, reflecting the adaptable nature of our emotional experiences and their potential to coexist. Our financial journey is fluid and dynamic, like driving on a highway, continuously changing lanes in response to the destination, road conditions, and surroundings. Similarly, we adjust our emotional drivers to cater to the various needs that we strive to fulfill at the same time.

The duality of money and the root of financial self-sabotage lies in the ways money can be used as a means to express security, power, freedom, and love. The relationship between emotions and money can of course be complex and multi-faceted. People's beliefs, experiences, and cultural backgrounds can significantly influence their behaviors. Therefore, getting to the root of financial self-sabotage is not linear, but understanding our emotional drivers is essential to advancing our financial potential.

To get to the root of Andrew's extracurricular spending —and to understand our own—we have to take a step back. Andrew's story is a good example in that we can see how the balance shifts throughout the earn, spend, save, give cycle, which is a universal truth for us all in our actions and motivations for money. Let's take a look at the yin and yang of each emotional driver, what extreme behavior looks like, and then look at how all four presented in Andrew's story.

Security

When the primary motivator for money matters is security, that's an indicator that there's a desire for stability, safety, and predictability. Like all of the emotional drivers, this influences one's attitudes and choices in earning, spending, saving, and giving money.

As with all the emotional drivers, the duality of security has two extremes. On the upside, acting with the motivation of security can lead to steady employment, benefits, and retirement; cautious spending, conservative investments, and an emergency fund. Security-motivated people make the most of their money and are focused on quality over quantity. Overall, this upside creates an immunity to financial gaps, troubles, or hiccups.

On the downside, acting with the motivation of security can lead to a person's complete risk aversion. In the extreme, this could lead to missed experiences and a diminished quality of life. Security and scarcity are first cousins, neither of whom we look forward to seeing at a family gathering.

At the beginning of Andrew's story, in his 20s, prior to receiving his inheritance, he and his wife lived on super-lean incomes as they were just starting out. They barely made ends meet, yet they did fine. Andrew told me, "It was almost a happier time because we knew exactly what was coming in, and we knew what we could mainly afford and not afford, hard stop." They were very prudent spenders, and were risk-averse, even as they came into inheritance. For 18 months after receiving the first big sum, they adhered to the strictest of financial regimens, not touching a penny of the inheritance. With security and predictability as the overarching driver, though, their quality of life wasn't the highest at that time. This upside-downside exemplifies the exact push-pull of the duality of money.

Power

A person who is motivated to use their money through the drive of feeling powerful often uses their money to influence an outcome. This can be political, social, familial, spiritual, relational, or cause-driven, and can have positive or negative impact. Money is used as leverage either to exert influence to get things done, easily pay to fix problems, and/or may be a source of a safety net to be able to make decisions without being overly vigilant or reliant on external forces. It's also a force for good in the world—contributing to causes that shape social change.

On the upside, a person using their money this way can follow their ambition, achieve a sense of control and leverage, and establish a legacy. They feel powerful, not powerless over money. Now, pursuing power for power's sake might lead to unethical behavior or choices, and power can overshadow moral and ethical considerations. In the extreme, I think of this in terms of the recipient. If the upside is influence, the other extreme for the recipient is abdication. If someone is under too much influence, they are, in effect, losing control. They are surrendering power and choice. They are following the influencer's direction, their wants, their way.

In Andrew's story, with the great responsibility of his inheritance, came great power. But for Andrew, in the beginning, he didn't know what to do with that power—or that responsibility. So his freedom motivation took over and, by default perhaps, he abdicated his power to explore who he was with this sudden influx of capital. While this fulfilled Andrew's need for connection, belonging, and meaning in his relationships, it fell short in nurturing his intrinsic motivation and overall well-being. His wellness, like all of ours, thrives on personal agency and the freedom to make independent choices.

Despite the deliberate choice to hold onto every single one of his pennies for dear life, Andrew felt like he was being controlled, and that's when he lost control—that's the duality of self-sabotage. In an effort to evade the feeling of being controlled internally, he went to the other extreme and spent wildly and impulsively. That was liberating, until it wasn't.

He almost had an unconscious blindness at first, while he followed the freedom motivation, and until it came back into balance and he started accepting and stepping into his true power and making conscious spending choices.

Freedom

When freedom is the primary emotional driver behind our money activities (earning, spending, saving, or giving), we enjoy a sense of liberation and independence. Freedom highlights Dr. Farkas' discussion of the human need for autonomy, so with freedom comes independence and autonomy to act as we wish, without the need to consult others in our choices.

The positive extreme of the drive for freedom is independence. People who are motivated by freedom may also be drawn to paths with more risk, driven by the potential for greater autonomy in their work, schedules, and financial outcomes. They may also choose to give money to causes that align with their values and feel empowered when they do. On the other end, then, when freedom is taken to the extreme, is isolation. An overemphasis on freedom can lead to strained relationships, neglecting responsibility, and impulsive risk-taking with harmful long-term consequences. In the extreme, freedom can lead to a kind of tunnel vision, and can take a toll on relationships, and that's where it can be isolating.

In Andrew's case, after 18 months of tightly restricted non-spending, Andrew's financial driver shifted from security to freedom. And this can happen to any of us with a promotion, salary increase, bonus payout, or—like my parents—a big sum payment. Suddenly, Andrew and his wife could afford anything they wanted. And in the beginning, they enjoyed the freedom of not having to worry about expenses.

But then the pendulum swung and their spending habits changed drastically—from spending next to nothing to blowing $30k a month for almost a year. Having watched every penny so closely for so long, it was as if they became immunized against inconvenience. This sudden overemphasis on independence put Andrew and his wife out of balance, and they shifted into neglecting responsibility, namely for their future planning and stability, including his daughter's college fund. At their new rate of spending, her college fund, which was sitting there right then, without intervention, would've been blown before she reached middle school. His autonomous spending spree was happening at the cost of his little girl's future. When that reality sunk in, he was able to make changes.

Love

People who are motivated to use their money to express love do so because they want to feel connected or needed.

One extreme of expressing love through money is enabling; the other extreme is dependence. One way to think about it is that if a person is giving money to feel connected, then they may subconsciously want to create a dependence, because that's how they get a guaranteed connection. In Andrew's case he "enabled" his family's every wish, never denying them anything they desired. Since he was reticent about the state of his finances, his family remained oblivious to the strain their demands placed on his resources. Unbeknownst to them, Andrew's consistent compliance placed the entire family's financial stability at risk.

The thing is, when each party is performing their action out of love—misplaced or misguided perhaps—they give money as an act of love and providing, and the recipient takes it to feel loved and provided for on some level. This is done with the best of intentions in the spirit of generosity and appreciation. And oftentimes, this is a beautiful exchange with no issues. Like all emotional drivers, it's when our feelings and actions are out of balance that the problem arises.

The duality of this is that giving and receiving is a way that we show love and feel love. These are highly correlated to the basic human needs of belonging and autonomy. The giver feels connected, yet in the extreme, is at the risk of ruining his or her financial future.

The receiver can build a dependency and diminished his capacity to stand on his own two feet, to choose a new direction (to make more money), or to accept life as it was. They can also feel bonded to the giver through their giving, but at the expense of their own autonomy.

The upside of the emotional money driver of love is that it can enhance the quality of one's life, provide a sense of joy, fulfillment, and a strengthened bond, as well as security. The downside is that a person motivated by love can set unrealistic expectations, cause financial strain, guilt, anxiety, and obsession, and lead to neglecting self-care.

Left unchecked, Andrew's spending would've literally bankrupted him. Fortunately, with some awareness, reflection, and recalibration, he brought it back into balance.

You're Not Alone

Understanding the full emotional picture, acknowledging our behaviors with money, and having meaningful conversations can help dispel the shrouds of secrecy and break down the walls of shame—precisely why this book exists. I'm so proud of Andrew, because after reflecting on his emotions and behaviors, and envisioning and acting on his desired future, he's on a different path—one with a secure future for his entire family, including his daughter's education.

It's All Inter-Related and We All Go through the Stages

What we can learn from the discussion of the emotional drivers (security, power, freedom, love) of our money actions (earn, save, spend, and give) is that building our self-awareness is essential to reaching our fullest financial potential. When we veer into acting in the extremes on our emotional money drivers or our money actions, our self-awareness and ability to have quality money conversations will save us from financial self-sabotage in the form of great losses.

It's as simple as that.

In my career, I've witnessed eight people, selflessly acting out of love, bankrupt themselves by giving everything to their very capable children. There are several more people who are on their path to blowing their earnings, savings, inheritance, retirement because their emotional drivers are out of balance. Andrew's story does us a great service in understanding how any of us can fluctuate in or out of any stage, changing our financial motivation, and therefore, changing our financial behavior, without much conscious thought about it. In other words, it's not hard to get caught off balance. Andrew's story also demonstrates how with awareness, reflection, and action, we can regain that balance and live our full potential.

Financial behavior is really sticky behavior, and it is not resolved by playing peek-a-boo with your bank accounts. It's not resolved by solely talking straight numbers, ever. When a person rebels financially, numbers by themselves won't change anything. But if you're on a fast track to depletion, a future snapshot of your story, such as, "Three years and seven months from today, your car(s) will be repossessed and you will be turning over your house keys because every dollar you have today, including your kid's college fund, will be gone," may have more impact. It's not about numbers. It's about potential consequences and feelings.

Financial advisors are trained to crunch numbers and give their best advice, and everyone lives happily ever after. Except, there are real humans involved with backgrounds and experiences and conflicting beliefs and emotions.

I learned early on, when logic and numbers don't move people forward in reaching their financial potential, it's an emotional matter. Understanding feelings and emotional drivers is where we can get people over the hump of self-sabotage. People don't care about numbers in a vacuum. What they care about is the story those numbers influence in terms of the feelings they are seeking. This includes you, dear reader. Take note if you are thinking, "Well, numbers don't excite me." Your future story, possibility, home, vacations, lifestyle, resources, and emotions likely do.

How to Self-Litigate out of the Extremes

What do we do when we find ourselves in the extremes—in an overemphasis of one of these emotional drivers and out of balance? And I say when, not if, because it will happen. Andrew's story demonstrates the continuum of change and fluctuation in the duality of money. It is possible to self-litigate through these stages—and that's not to say I suggest you do it solo. That's to suggest that it starts with self-awareness. We'll discuss how to cultivate that in upcoming chapters.

Just like all four of these drivers appeared at different times in different extremes and were present in Andrew's evolution, different versions of the same story happen for most of us. Receiving a lump sum through inheritance or bonus or salary increase, hanging on tight to our dough, and completely rebelling are recurring themes that I see often in my practice.

You absolutely can learn to be good with money and learn your own balance indicators through the work in this book.

Keeping secrets of what we do and don't do with our money, and how we feel about it, are outdated concepts. They are behaviors handed down generation to generation, and no longer serve our best interests. That includes you. After this set of exercises to uncover what emotions are driving your decisions and actions, we'll explore your moneyhood.

Money Motivations Exercises

If you've seen a child's first joyous glimpse of the ocean, felt valued receiving a thank-you gift, thrown money at a problem, or paid for an upgrade, then you're familiar with the emotions of security, power, freedom, and love, and understand how money impacts others and drives us. This also means you pursue experiences and feelings that are beyond money's reach. Many of us do (this is normal)— whether it's *Sex and the City* vibes with Manolos, a surgical path to the fountain of youth, partying like it's 1999, or simply giving to a good cause.

To help contextualize your thinking, consider ways you use money to enhance your well-being, influence, or your standing with other people. How does money motivation (security, power, freedom, or love) appear in your life?

Do you ...

- overspend on gifts?
- spend or save an IRS tax refund?
- track every penny you earn or spend?
- buy two pairs of shoes, not one, when shopping with friends?
- settle for less rather than go for it?
- invest in yourself?
- pay for access or conveniences?
- give yourself permission to pursue (and pay for) your dreams?

1. Which emotional driver is most influential in your financial decisions right now?
2. What's beneath the situations and/or people that trigger you?

3. Has chasing a feeling ever led to financial self-sabotage? personal fulfillment?
4. What might you need to heal, stop doing, or do more of to realize your full financial potential?

4

Your Moneyhood

*I*n order to lay the foundation to reach your full financial potential, it is important to examine the past. This helps us understand anything keeping us silent and scared in our money matters. Reflecting on our beliefs —what they are, where they came from, and whether they are really ours—and recalling our most formative memories around money—financial flashpoints, moneyisms, and understanding how they may anchor our money beliefs— will help us make sense of our formative financial experiences.

For me, the marina moment was certainly a financial plot twist. However, it wasn't my first formative moment. For that, we have to go back further—back to our earliest memories of *talking* about money.

Mine happened when I was five. I had just woken up in my bottom bunk bed, wearing my Sesame Street jammies with purple barrettes in my hair, and was looking forward to cartoons. My father strolled in, looked at the glass jar of coins on top of my dresser, and asked if he could borrow some money.

"What's it for?" It wasn't like I was saving up for anything special. I only put them there because I saw my mom doing the same thing with her coins in her room. I asked because I was curious.

"Cigarettes," he said.

I recoiled at the thought of being part of this thing that I knew made your lungs black, stunk up the house, and killed people.

"No." I don't think he anticipated his little girl would be that bold.

He shot me a look somewhere between exasperation and disgust, reached into my jar, and took my money anyway.

I burst into tears. Full-on waterworks of heaving sobs salted with hurt and confusion.

He looked at me, turned on his heel, and walked out with my money in his hands. Without a word.

Immediately, I felt the sting of dismissal. I wanted a do-over.

No, no, no. You can have my money.

I take back what I said.

I wanted to run after him and to take back my words, in the hope of feeling loved and approved of, but I was frozen and unable to speak.

I couldn't name then how horrible it felt to be played in his sick game of "pretend permission": asking and then doing what he wanted to anyway. That he went against my wishes made me feel and think things that I didn't know how to name or express, much less understand, as a five-year-old. And neither evidently could my father, so he gave me the silent treatment for standing up for my values.

Financial Flashpoints

This memory, tattooed onto my brain, is what's called a financial flashpoint. I was a bystander who got tangled up in my father's ideas of what money, love, boundaries, and agency over one's own financial choices mean. I worried that he thought I was being stingy, when in truth, I was looking out for him. I wondered if he knew I loved him too much to want to be a part of buying a harmful pack of cigarettes. Worst of all, I blamed myself that he left me alone with my tears. And yes, all of these thoughts went through my tiny, young noggin.

Flashpoints are emotionally charged, life-changing moments that positively or negatively shock the system and have the power to change strongly held beliefs in an instant. They create an emotional, cognitive, and visceral memory in the body that records the experience, often leading to later-life flashbacks. What happened to me instantly taught me to believe that it didn't matter what I wanted to do with my money. At that moment, I became a *financial people pleaser*. I was stunned into silence—and didn't speak up much from that point forward.

Silence and secrecy around money is a common theme for all of us, rooted in cultural history and family dynamics. It's not so much that we resist talking about money, it's that we resist talking about our feelings about money.

When left unresolved, anything that reminds us of a flashpoint has the unconscious potential to keep us frozen in time. This happens when we project unresolved feelings onto money, and use it as an emotional outlet by attempting to buy things that money cannot buy—like status, love, or confidence. Money is an enabler on which we are codependent to underwrite much of what's important in life. Take it from me, money does not buy closure or healing or inner peace. Only talking about money does that, but I'm getting ahead of myself. Right now we are uncovering our secrets, so that *later* we can release them by talking about them more fruitfully.

Moneyisms

Parents say the darndest things. Perhaps growing up, you heard, "Must be nice," as if money was meant for other people, not us; or "That's none of your business, young lady," as in we don't ask or talk about money. How these phrases landed on your ears has a lot to do with how you think and act with your money today.

We all heard money expressions growing up, or moneyisms as I like to call them. Think of moneyisms as the financial equivalent of telegrams or today's instant messaging. These phrases convey certain ideas or attitudes that gradually assimilate into our minds. Depending on the context, intention, tone, and veracity of what was said and heard, moneyisms are how our parents directly and indirectly communicated their money beliefs, preferences, and attitudes on everything from credit to wealth. They can be things like, "Who do you think we are, the Rockefellers?" or "Hey, money doesn't grow on trees," or "Only if we can get it on sale." Moneyisms are often an invisible force to be reckoned with. They can feel like something outside of our control is in charge and keeps us from getting what we want.

In his twenties, my client EJ was the Gordon Gekko type. You know, the Wall Street hotshot in the movie with the slicked-back hair and the "Greed is good" mantra. Lured by the prospect of making big money, he took a job as an investment banker straight out of graduate school. Five years into his career he was making bank. So, EJ had

a good job and was making great money, yet he had zip—
nothing to show for all the long hours and hard work he'd
put in.

Wondering where it all went? Think clubs, limos, and
high-end entertainment. If there was something to buy, he
didn't think twice; it was his. When you're dealing with the
kind of cash EJ made, the sky's the limit for self-
indulgence.

He was a smart guy who couldn't figure out how to get
a handle on his money. With the help of a therapist, he
explored what was holding him back. That's when he
remembered his father's financial mantra, "Money isn't
important." "Money isn't important," is something his
father repeated over and over when EJ was a kid.

He heard it but never realized it seeped in and that he
internalized that belief subconsciously. Literally, yesterday's
moneyism became EJ's operating system. EJ had been
treating money like it wasn't important, just like his dad
said, and out the door it went. Adding fuel to the fire, the
belief about money transferred to his job, as well. He hated
being an investment banker, and was angry, upset, and
confused that he was broke.

When adult EJ re-wrote the moneyism to be "Money
isn't everything, but it is important," things changed. EJ
started treating it, and himself, with respect. He worked
with a recruiter, quit Wall Street, and changed jobs almost
immediately. He was able to become intentional about his
financial choices. Over time, he nurtured a healthy relationship into existence. And while he made less income at
first, his star gradually rose and he eventually surpassed
what he'd been making as a banker—only this time, he
saved.

The key to EJ's transformation was rewriting the
moneyism of "Money isn't important," to "Money isn't

everything, but it is important." Over time, EJ built a successful business as a sports agent, met and married the love of his life, started a family, and created a life he loves.

This transformation is available to all of us when we examine our moneyisms, and how they affect us today.

Our Moneyhood

Financial flashpoints and moneyisms, like all formative financial experiences, contribute to our moneyhood. Our moneyhood is made up of social, emotional, cultural, and financial experiences we grew up with that affect our financial choices and behaviors throughout our lives. You can think of your moneyhood like your neighborhood—it's where you grew up, financially.

As much as I loved my parents, trouble was brewing long before the moment on the marina dock. When their moving business expanded to relocate military personnel from base to base, jobs would take months to receive payment, resulting in large backlogs of accounts receivable.

As Mom and Dad waited for large government balances to be paid, these payments turned into a kind of pseudo-savings account. There was just one problem. When the check came in, they immediately cashed them and spent every penny. Literally. Every penny.

This pattern of making large purchases with the sudden influx of cash became a hallmark of my parents' relationship with money.

Essentially, the larger the payment, the bigger the toys. The bigger the toys, the harder it was to maintain the lifestyle we were projecting to the rest of the world, and the more my mother scraped by. We barely made ends meet at home.

Regardless of all the hard work and high income, my parents were always within an inch of bouncing checks. Despite having a large house, sports cars, and private airplanes, we were actually broke. At one point, we were so behind on the mortgage, that the bank started foreclosing on our house. At another point, although we had a brand new Corvette, we did not have health insurance.

For a long time, I had no awareness of our financial precarity. Young children don't know the difference between big expenses and small ones. As children, most of us have the luxury of assuming that our parents know what they are doing with their money. I was no exception.

I was ten years old when I found out otherwise. One day I returned home from school early and found my mother crying into a shoebox full of envelopes. Each envelope was meant for a particular household bill. She couldn't afford any of them.

My mother explained that my father's expensive toys had been paid for out of large lump sums, and there wasn't any money left over. The mortgage was long past due and the bank was threatening to foreclose. In addition, we owed past years of income taxes and penalties to the IRS.

This conversation terrified me. I did my best to calm my mother; I became her financial confidant, and over the years she told me everything. In psychological terms, my mother "enmeshed" me in their financial struggles, telling me things because it helped to relieve her stress. Her worries became my worries, creating a profound sense of insecurity in me. I began to feel an ever-present, invisible threat that someday it could all disappear.

Being exposed to this kind of financial stress as a child was like breathing second-hand smoke. You take in the carcinogens with no way to exhale. You can't control any part of it, but you are damaged by the exposure.

In October of my senior year in high school, I had a cold that progressively worsened. This was the 80s, pre-HMO era, when doctor's office visits and prescriptions were paid out of pocket, and my mom was worried about being able to afford a checkup. She thought I'd feel better soon, but hope wasn't the right strategy. On New Year's Eve, while my parents were at a party, I stayed home—the weakest and most "off" I'd ever felt in my life.

When my temperature hit 103, I called the party host's landline, asked for my mother, and delivered an ultimatum; either she and my father come home and take me to the hospital or I was calling an ambulance. They came home ultimately, drove me to the ER, and I was hospitalized for two weeks with mono. Amidst the backdrop of our large house, MG replica, TransAm, Chevy Camaro, and Honda Acura, our finances were channeled into a new Cessna for a Disney trip instead of securing health insurance, leading to such unnecessary drama.

Money took on an air of life or death. The hardest part was maintaining the facade of wealth and ease. No one outside of our family knew about our money concerns or that instead of health insurance premiums, my parents were making car payments and gambling on when the next big government check would land. Everyone in our family understood that it was verboten to speak about our concerns outside of our house.

And, in fact, we weren't talking about it in any productive way inside our house either. But we did argue about it. Arguing about money is not talking about money, but if there were arguments about money in your household, take note: these are modern-day moneyisms for you, and need to be excavated.

Moneyhood Builds Our Relationship with Money

Flashpoints and moneyisms are formative; they influence our relationship with money. I call the set of stories, beliefs, and behaviors that we get from our childhood part of "our moneyhood." It's important to recall and record these stories if we are going to properly process and heal them. We will do this together in just a moment.

There are numerous factors that contribute to our adult beliefs, attitudes, and financial behaviors, such as family dynamics and intergenerational transfer of beliefs. Additionally, factors like conflict, communication styles, gender socialization, cultural influences, social comparison, socioeconomic status, our biology, and financial culture also play significant roles.

Acknowledging the significance of these factors in the overall picture, this book focuses on the six transformational concepts that have the most direct and immediate impact on your financial life and moneyhood. They are: financial flashpoints, moneyisms, secrecy bias, moneyself (our identity), emotional drivers, and money scripts.

Our moneyhood sets the tone for our financial behaviors. If it's positive, we approach money with abundance and hope. If we have a negative moneyhood, we approach money with fear and scarcity. This can be happening subconsciously, and we want to examine that, because if you're not where you most want to be, it's possible to change it.

It starts with your moneyhood. *Everyone has one.*

To assess your moneyhood, and to get a start on seeing how it may have laid a path for your subconscious beliefs and habits today, grab a journal, your CSI analyst mindset, and complete the following prompts.

Moneyhood Exercises

1. Flashpoints

Let's settle into your *most* pivotal financial flashpoint. Spill the tea. What exactly happened? Did your heart soar or sink? What changed in your life from that moment forward? And how did the adults who hovered around your universe react? Were they pillars of wisdom, or did they crumble like a cookie?

How does this defining moment play a role in your financial decisions today? In what ways is the flashpoint a cautionary tale or the blueprint of your success?

2. Moneyisms

What were those moneyisms that played on repeat in the jukebox of your upbringing? "Money doesn't grow on trees?" "A penny saved is a penny earned?" "Your money's no good here!" Jot them down.

How does it feel digging those up? Like a casual stroll down memory lane or more like pulling teeth? What did you think the sender of those moneyisms meant at the time? More importantly, how have you carried them into your financial life today? Are they little guardian angels whispering wisdom, or have they become gremlins nibbling away at your financial well-being?

3. A Creative Stretch: Your Moneyisms Licensing Deal

Imagine that you've been offered a licensing deal to use your personal moneyisms on a line of tee-shirts, mugs, journals, tote bags, and candles—the works. Knowing that your moneyisms could become someone else's financial guideposts, including your own, what would you choose: ones you grew up with or something else? Write down three moneyisms for your licensing deal and why you chose them. Here are some examples to get you started.

From:	To:
Money is the root of all evil.	Money is just a tool.
More (money) is better.	The best things in life are free.
Money is power.	I'm powerful with money.
Money corrupts.	Money is a force for good.
Don't spend it all in one place!	Invest in what sparks joy.
It's all about the Benjamins.	It's all about my values, not my valuables.
Time is money.	Time is limited. Money is abundant.
It takes money to make money.	Great wealth is built from scratch.
Money doesn't grow on trees.	My wealth comes from my relationships.

5

Money Scripts

*a*s you learn about how your money beliefs emerge from your life experiences, your bias for secrecy, flashpoints, moneyisms, financial self-sabotage, and the development of your moneyself, it may begin to feel like your money beliefs are as unique as your DNA. While that is partially true, it is also the case that there are some money beliefs that emerge in person after person. These common beliefs have been described by Dr. Brad Klontz and Dr. Sonya Britt as money scripts.

Like a movie script, money scripts dictate how we act: they tell us how to respond in different money scenarios, dictate what we say, and they inform how we make our choices. Money scripts are learned in childhood, often unconscious, passed down through the generations, just partial truths, and at the same time, responsible for our financial outcomes.

The primary money scripts described by Drs. Klontz and Britt describe four desires that drive the way we approach money.

Desire: Matching Money Script

1. To avoid money issues: money avoidance
2. To accumulate money: money focus
3. To differentiate ourselves from other socioeconomic classes: money status
4. To keep one's money issues private: money vigilance

Before we go any further, I recommend that you take the free money scripts quiz to better understand what drives *your* behavior and what your dominant money script is.

Money scripts, as measured by the Klontz Money Script® Inventory-Revised (KMSI-R) are linked to factors such as income, net worth, credit card debt, financial behaviors, and other important aspects of financial health.

The results of this quiz will help you assess your personal money strengths and recognize and work with your existing beliefs. For many people, this is an important step toward increasing income and net worth, and improving financial health. Don't get caught up on the labels themselves because, no matter what the money script inventory says, you can absolutely improve your money management style and take strides toward your full financial potential.

Here's a QR Code, where you can take the free quiz and receive your results by email.

After completing the money script inventory, you probably noticed that you relate to some or maybe even all of these money scripts. That's normal.

In my practice with this tool, I've found that people will *really* resonate with one or two of the scripts, and these will be the ones that impact you the most. Some of them can be traced right back to flashpoints and moneyisms we learned in our families of origin—but don't be surprised if some of your beliefs can't be traced back to anything. Sometimes we pick up beliefs, like barnacles on a boat, from unusual places—friends' parents, movies we saw, or books we don't even remember reading. Regardless of where they came from, once we identify these beliefs, we can evaluate whether they are serving us.

Money Scripts and Potential Pitfalls

Since we know that our money beliefs affect our financial behaviors, it's important to bring attention to the ways in which your money scripts might be affecting your behaviors. The first three money scripts—(1) money avoidance, (2) money focus, and (3) money status—are associated with poorer financial health, including lower net worth and lower income.

By contrast, those scoring high on the fourth money script—(4) money vigilance—tend toward cost consciousness (i.e., frugality). They see saving as important, are discreet about money matters, and feel nervous about making sure money is saved for emergencies.

Wherever you land in this assessment, it will provide important clues on where you may need specific support. As a financial advisor, I use this tool regularly to help me get to know new clients. For example, I have a client who scored high on the money avoidance scale. In fact, she has admitted to me that she does not ever look at any financial information. As a result, I know that our meetings may be her only feedback loop. When discussing her money, I'm careful not to overwhelm her with information that she is not up-to-date on, while still getting the point across about whether she is financially on or off track. Once you know your own money scripts, you can be equally strategic with yourself.

Here are the main behaviors to watch out for in each money script:

Money Avoidance

Money avoiders are characterized by beliefs like:

- I do not deserve money.
- Good people shouldn't care about money.
- Money corrupts people.

When one holds beliefs like these, they unknowingly sabotage their financial success or give money away in an unconscious effort to have as little as possible. This may happen even as they may be working excessive hours in an effort to make money.

Not surprisingly, money avoidance is associated with poor financial health; money avoiders tend to have less money and lower net worth. In addition, it can be associated with an increased risk of overspending and compulsive buying, sacrificing one's financial well-being for the sake of others, and avoiding looking at one's bank or credit card statements, and never consulting their budgets (if they even have one). These habits all indicate that a person is trying to forget about his or her financial situation.

Money avoidance example:

Tara came to me having already worked through the worst of her money avoidance. As a child, she had lived very close to the poverty level, and her family spent some time on welfare and using food stamps. As an adult, she earned a PhD and achieved a level of income that is best described as "upper middle class," which to her felt indescribably rich.

By the time she began working with me, Tara had worked through some of her most egregious money beliefs, like, "People like me don't care about money," and "Money corrupts relationships."

However, Tara was still struggling with the behavioral aspects of money. She didn't want to look at her credit card bills, she got anxious when looking at a budget, and spent more money than was wise on eating out and buying cosmetics. When we sat down to talk about these remaining vestiges of her money avoidance mindset, we hit on a deeply-held belief that was keeping her locked in money avoidance.

As a mother of two young children and a lifelong fan of children's television, she described this belief as the Scrooge McDuck comparison. Essentially, as a child of poor parents with very few role models of middle and upper middle class money management, Tara was comparing herself to the only rich person she had as a reference—Scrooge McDuck.

Scrooge, as you may know, is the richest duck in the world and keeps his money as coins in a vault he is inexplicably able to swim through. Scrooge, though very frugal, didn't need to be careful with his money at all. My client said this, about the Scrooge McDuck comparison, "I realized that while I was intimately familiar with all the different ways a person could be poor, I was stuck with just one understanding of being rich. I thought that when I would have 'enough' money, all my financial problems would go away. I thought I'd be swimming in money, and able to do whatever I wanted."

But this wasn't Tara's experience. Even though she and her husband made more than "enough money" as a family, they didn't feel they were able to do whatever they wanted. In other words, they weren't experiencing the abundance of the money they were bringing in. "We can't take international trips or go to Disney World, or buy a new car every few years. This discrepancy, the fact that we had money, but were still plagued by scarcity, made me feel like I had done something really wrong. It wasn't until I realized that there are at least as many ways to be financially secure as there were to be financially insecure, that I started managing my money in a more matter of fact way. Essentially, I had to let go of my inner Scrooge McDuck."

Money Focus

For the money focused, beliefs like these dominate their relationship with money:

- You can never have enough money.

- More money would solve all my problems.
- More money would make me happier.

The tension between believing that more money and more material things will make one happier and the sense that one will never have enough money can result in chronic overspending in an attempt to buy happiness.

Those who focus on money are more likely to have lower income, lower net worth, and be trapped in a cycle of revolving credit card debt. Money focusers are also more likely to spend compulsively, hoard possessions, put work ahead of their relationships, and be financially dependent on others.

Money Focus example:

Julie's parents told her that she'd never have to worry a day in her life about money. Her parents set up a trust fund for her—enough to last a lifetime, she was told. Her father passed away unexpectedly when she was in grade school. While provisions had been made for Julie, nothing was left to her mother. With no other way to support them, Julie's mother used the trust fund to provide for them both. As Julie planned her wedding, her mother fessed up to what she had done. By then, there was very little left in the trust fund.

So the "enough to last a lifetime" promise turned out to be a gross overstatement. Julie went from feeling secure and carefree about money to being a money-focused workaholic. She chased promotions and new assignments all around the world and clung to the climb up the corporate ladder as a means to recreate the security she felt as a little girl. Julie had the deeply held belief that "Money will fix all of my problems." In order to budge from this rigid, money focus script, Julie would have some inner work to do.

The challenge is, money focus can lead to workaholism. The key advice is to focus on relationships, connecting, spending time with loved ones, and chosen hobbies, as well as practicing gratitude to cultivate a sense of enough.

Money Status

People focused on money status carry beliefs like:

- I will not buy something unless it is new.
- Poor people are lazy.
- Your self-worth equals your net worth.

People with money status beliefs may pretend to have more money than they do in an effort to give others the impression that they are financially successful. As a result, those with a focus on money status are more likely to be compulsive spenders. Because they are worried that others may find out the truth, they may lie to their closest friends, and even their spouses about their spending. Holding the money status script is also predictive of an addiction to gambling, as individuals may gamble in an attempt to win large sums of money to prove their worth to themselves and others.

Money Status example:

Growing up, Rachel internalized the message, "You can't have *both* love and money"—or the shoes, or anything else you may need, unless you perform to certain standards. Raised by a mother who only gave her money based on perfect performances, she felt like a "trained animal at the circus" who had to sing for her supper. In her money-hood, money and love felt nearly interchangeable, tightly regulated, and always closely connected to feeling controlled.

Save for the early part of her career, there were good reasons that Rachel ran her own consulting agency and didn't work for big companies. In her words, because "I would just tell them to shove it." Corporate work subconsciously boxed her in as her mother once had.

As an entrepreneur, she loved calling her own shots, but her upbringing had confused her sense of self-worth for her net-worth. As a result, Rachel had difficulty charging appropriately for her services. She was afraid if she charged "too much" her clients would reject her—in her emotional experience, they wouldn't love her. She thought she had to "perform." Under-charging and over-delivering just about guaranteed she would receive the love and approval from her clients that she desperately wanted from her mother.

She made her big money breakthrough when she recognized that she had been waiting to be rewarded for her work (as her mother had done), rather than charging upfront for the value she provided to her clients. She now submits proposals at three times her previous rates, and clients don't bat an eye. More importantly, Rachel feels worthy of receiving both love and money.

Money Vigilance

The money vigilant are alert, watchful, and concerned about their financial welfare, holding beliefs such as:

- I would be a nervous wreck if I didn't have money saved for an emergency.

- You should always look for the best deal before you buy something, even if it takes more time.
- You should not tell others how much money you have or make.
- People shouldn't take financial handouts.

People who are vigilant about their money believe it is important to save and for people to work for their money and not be given financial handouts. If they can't pay cash for something, they won't buy it, and they are less likely to buy on credit.

As a result, the money vigilant have higher incomes and higher net worths. While they can be anxious and secretive about their financial status with people outside their closest relationships, they are less likely to lie to their spouse about spending behaviors. They are also significantly less likely to spend compulsively, gamble excessively, enable others financially, and ignore their finances.

Such an approach encourages saving and frugality, which are positive traits. However, when on overload, it can lead to excessive wariness, anxiety, and secrecy, and can impede the growth of wealth. Money vigilance is hindered by a commitment to secrecy and an unwillingness to talk about money openly that stalls the growth of wealth and financial security that we desire. As discussed in chapter 2, my experience reveals that our bias toward secrecy causes the biggest failures in our financial health. This is especially true when someone with money vigilance is in a relationship with people carrying the other money scripts.

Without a willingness to discuss money freely and communicate frankly about differences of opinion, one partner's money vigilance can be overwhelmed by the other's beliefs. If, on the other hand, both partners learn to speak freely about money (a particularly difficult task for the money vigilant), they can pursue money goals as a team.

Money Vigilance example:

Lisa's voice cracked as she told me, "On one hand, I feel like I should be satisfied with what I'm making, but on the other hand, I know I'm not being paid fairly." She knew others in her role were making more. And she knew asking for a raise made sense, yet felt as if an invisible force was keeping her from doing so.

Raised by a single mom who struggled to get by, she worried about money a lot as a child. She worked from a young age, never accepting help because "I knew what it felt like not to have enough," and "preferred to give to others." Research confirms that "prosocial" behavior like giving money to others makes us happy, which Lisa learned first-hand as a young girl. Yet, in an interesting twist, she adopted the belief growing up that "People should work and not be given financial handouts."

When we know rationally and logically we should do something and don't, that's a clue that something deeper is going on—usually a limiting belief. In this case, the belief was "People should not be given handouts."

The "invisible force" stopping Lisa was that she had confused the idea of negotiating for a raise with asking for a handout. Once she understood the irrational link between the two, she was set free. "I work hard for the money" took on a whole new meaning as she met with her manager and scored an increase on par with her counterparts.

From a money script perspective, people who are money vigilant tend to need coaching to spend and enjoy their money because their belief is that money is meant to be saved, not spent, and they like their rainy day funds. Advice for money vigilant people is to plan their splurges to enjoy some of their money. It often helps if they enjoy their money with others, give to causes, and/or do things with people they love.

In Lisa's case, my advice would be to ask for the raise, then give some of the money to people in need.

Rethink and Rewrite Your Money Script

Regardless of your dominant money script style—avoidance, focus, status, or vigilance—what's important is that you are increasing your self-knowledge and self-awareness. This is a critical component to auditing your script, and if desired, tweaking it for more optimal outcomes. Big things can happen with small changes, and small changes start with self-awareness.

Understanding my father's money script helped me understand my own and others' better. Dad is a textbook operator of a money status script. He cashed in my college fund and bought himself a yacht and named that yacht *Another Toy*, after all. The technical belief about the money status script is the unconscious belief that "My self-worth equals my net-worth." That always felt incomplete and too shallow to explain or understand my father's motivations.

What's occurred to me is that my father was subconsciously driven to belong. He bought all kinds of toys to show that he fit in; that he belonged. I believe the mental crowd he was trying to fit in with was his father and uncles who were big, larger-than-life influences in his life, successful and showy in their own ways as well. I'm reminded again how my friend Howard Farkas taught me that self-sabotage arises from an imbalance between two universal human needs: belonging and autonomy. This insight feels right from a cellular level to me.

It's insights like these that have furthered my processing of my parents' financial betrayal and allowed me to heal, and in turn, use these insights and experience to help others do the same.

Money Script Exercises

Below, we'll dive into more specifics about your money tendencies and how your scripts are serving you (or not), and what you can do about it.

- First, take the money scripts quiz. Its valuable insights will be of great impact to your self-knowledge.

- Journal on your thoughts about the money scripts assessment. Does it describe you accurately or miss the mark? Why is that? Do you see yourself in more than one script? Is there a certain story, a defining flashpoint, or a moneyism that makes you agree or disagree with the question statements?

Money Script Categories

1. Money Avoidance: Can you identify three sticky money-related situations or decisions in your life where you steer clear of or procrastinate taking action?
2. Money Focus: Reflect on your financial goals and habits. Do you find yourself fixating on

accumulating money as a priority over relationships or health?

3. Money Status: Consider your beliefs and actions related to status. Do you ever find yourself comparing your yoga mat to your neighbor's? Does this ever lead you to splurge or regret?

4. Money Vigilance: Do you maintain a strict fortress of solitude and secrecy around your financial affairs? Does your knack for keeping quiet ever affect your financial security and decision-making?

Beliefs: Jot down three beliefs you realize aren't doing you any favors.

Circle one to work on changing (we'll talk about how in chapter 8).

6

Your Moneyself

*W*hat made my parents forego necessities and binge-spend on a Cessna and a Jag? What makes anyone spend the way they do? We've talked about our moneyhood, which is our money environment: the social, emotional, cultural, and financial neighborhood we grow up in. This creates an ever-changing, fluid state of mind in adulthood that affects our financial choices and behaviors throughout our lives.

Now we will be more specific to our individual self. When we talk about the collection of beliefs we have about ourselves as adults, we are really referring to our identity, or our self.

When it comes to our finances, it's all about our "moneyself," my term for our money identity. Since my parents' new yacht sank my college plans, I've made it my life's mission to understand what shapes our financial attitudes and values and what drives our behaviors. We aren't born with them. No one pops out of the womb quoting Adam Smith, the father of modern economics, with theories that form the basis of capitalism as we know it. And yet, by adulthood, we are full of beliefs, in every category of life.

The same concepts are echoed within ourselves, our parents, colleagues, and friends. I see the potential in all of us to identify and change our beliefs about money—if we want to. It's not as hard as one may think, perhaps because the exchange of money is an external act with visible consequences.

Beyond money, we hold beliefs about what it means to be human, such as:

- It's important to be kind.
- Family comes first.
- We should respect our elders.

Beliefs around money itself may include moneyisms, such as:

- Hard work is important.
- Save before you spend.
- Money isn't everything.
- You only live once, so spend it while you got it.

These beliefs shape our behaviors and create our habits, which contribute to our moneyself. They define what we value, they guide the advice we give others, and they frame how we live our lives.

One way to think about beliefs is that they are the outcome of our socialization. This includes cultural beliefs such as race, gender, and socioeconomic status. These beliefs emerge from our lived experience of the world we live in. For example, maybe "society" claims that women are bad at math. If you've internalized this belief, you may avoid math and are impeded in your financial goals for this reason.

Even if you vehemently disagree with this concept, however, and have worked to disprove it by becoming excellent at math yourself, it is still impacting you. In this case, societal belief impacts your life by prompting you to overcome it. In this way, societal beliefs influence us whether we agree or disagree with them. Similarly, beliefs that come from our personal experiences impact us in interesting and dynamic ways.

In my own experience, I witnessed a lifetime of reckless decisions with far-reaching consequences. I learned many beliefs through those experiences.

- As a child, I learned that money can appear and disappear at a moment's notice.
- As a teenager, I learned that money can create an alluring illusion of luxury to the world, while the truth might be entirely different at home.
- And on the dock of that marina, just before college, I learned that you can't count on anyone else to help you financially.

Beliefs Are Entirely Changeable

While some of these beliefs are still very much intact, other beliefs have changed significantly as I've gotten older and (I hope) wiser. That's the interesting thing about beliefs: they feel like the truth when we believe them, but they are often entirely changeable.

At their core, money problems—like all human problems—involve complications of the mind. Everything from overeating to failing to communicate with a romantic partner can be traced back to a set of beliefs guiding us to behave in ways that don't support our goals. This means if you want to enact real behavior change, create healthier habits, and satisfy your self-improvement commitments, you have to change your mind, literally.

"Change your mind to change your life" can sound concurrently like a foregone conclusion and a pipe-dream. This is because we *know* that we are often our own worst enemy when it comes to money. And yet, we have lived through countless failed efforts to change who we are in the name of "self-improvement."

I want to help you change the conversation around your money beliefs. First, it is not necessary to change who we are in order to create financial security. Instead, we need to better understand ourselves. Then, with that deeper understanding, we can use our existing strengths to build new beliefs that are entirely in line with *who we have always been.*

Now, we will explore where our initial beliefs come from, referencing our earliest money experiences as we've already talked about, our financial flashpoints, and our moneyhood: the social, emotional, cultural, and financial experiences we grew up with.

We will examine how our experiences shaped our beliefs and consistent actions, and consider whether they are serving our greater good, or not.

The Creation of the "Moneyself"

The basis of our entire identity, including the foundation of our moneyself, from a psychological perspective, is formed in childhood. Children absorb more by listening to conversations, reading facial expressions, watching body language, and observing interactions between the adults in their lives than they will ever learn from books or formal lessons.

All this input from our immediate environment combines to create unexamined beliefs.

These are then examined and solidified in adolescence. James Marcia, the theorist most associated with identity formation, describes a four-stage process that helps us to understand how we end up with fervent and entrenched beliefs about ourselves and, for the purpose of reaching your full financial potential, our money.

Stage 1: Childhood and Diffused Beliefs

During childhood, we all notice money and become curious about it. In the beginning, it's little more than a mysterious, inanimate object we observe our parents and other adults using to get things they want or need. For most children, few words are spoken to us about money and so, we haven't created any emotional connections with it yet— we are just soaking it all in like the naive sponges we are.

Still, even as we absorb the sights and sounds around us, our money sense is forming. This describes how most beliefs are formed in childhood (such as our moneyself): they begin in "diffusion" which is when we have a lot of latent and unexamined beliefs. We certainly do have beliefs, and they are guiding our actions and impacting our relationships, but we don't really know what they are.

As an example, let's say that your mother and father struggled to make ends meet. You remember heated conversations behind closed doors, doors slamming, crying, and maybe the silent treatment. These experiences during your childhood formed the latent beliefs that "Talking about money is stressful," and "Money isn't something you discuss in front of children." Neither of these beliefs is conscious, and yet they would cause you to be surprised if a friend's father discusses money in front of you, or if someone talks about money without complaining.

Stage 2: Adolescence and Foreclosure of Strong Beliefs

When we enter adolescence, many of our latent beliefs are brought forward into our conscious mind, examined, and transformed into our conscious, adult beliefs. Some of them are accepted exactly as they are. In that process, they enter the phase of identity development called "foreclosure." A little different than the more commonly used definition in real estate, this foreclosure rules out or prevents a course of action. These are usually the beliefs that are held most strongly by the family of origin.

Related to money, most people are in the identity-foreclosure state because it's such an unexamined area of life. (More naval gazing please!) Identity-foreclosure status is the status for those who have made a commitment to an identity without having explored options. In other words, we just accept what has been presented—moneyisms, observations, traditions, zeitgeist, experiences—and we commit to whatever we made them mean at that time, without considering alternatives.

From Marcia's *Theory of Identity Development*, "...latent beliefs are brought forward into our conscious mind, examined, and transformed into our conscious, adult beliefs," which is a fancy way of saying that teenagers (adolescents) question, explore, and rebel as a way of ultimately forming their identity.

Beliefs that come from religion, for example, often slide right in without being critically examined because questioning them feels too risky, or it feels like a waste of time because the belief feels self-obvious. Families with strong money legacies, either about "What it means to be poor," or "We are rich and that means this kind of responsibility," could have children who have a moneyself that is largely in foreclosure.

For example, the experience of standing on the sidewalk with a U-Haul truck behind you, looking at your home's "sold" sign, as your mother tries not to cry next to you, might have been so traumatizing that it seems self-obvious to you that "Money can disappear and your life can be upended entirely at seemingly any time." Some of our beliefs, like this one, are felt so strongly that they feel self-evident and often remain in foreclosure until another flashpoint (or flashback) forces us to re-evaluate them.

Stage 3: Later Adolescence: Critical Examination

Later in adolescence, we are likely to critically examine many beliefs about money. When this happens, we become aware of our belief and then ask, "But is that true?" This is one of the reasons that adults find adolescents so confronting. Adolescents are hardwired to ask, "Why?" and then debate or argue with what they hear. Marcia calls this time of intense exploration, before the person commits to a belief, "moratorium."

For example, it might be that your parents were fond of saying, "It's more important to save for a rainy day than to have the newest gadgets," but your experience with financial insecurity has you wondering if in fact, "You only live once, so we should spend it while we've got it," is closer to what you believe.

While in this critical examination or moratorium stage, we will try out different behaviors, like cycling between spending all of our money, trying to save, and wondering if it's possible to split the difference somehow, and will almost certainly be arguing with our parents, insisting that they "don't understand us at all."

Stage 4: Adulthood: Incorporated Beliefs

Identity achievement is the term Marcia uses when a belief becomes incorporated into our adult identity. If we have good role models who are willing to speak with us honestly and in depth about money, we may "achieve" healthy money beliefs that serve us well.

Unfortunately, most of what parents actually say to their children about money reveals little about their thoughts and decision-making processes. It's not that they never talk about money. Rather, most conversations with children about money are at the surface-level.

As wonderful as it would be, rare are the parents who create PowerPoint decks and sit their children down for a series of "money talks" as they grow up. Instead, we're mostly left to figure all of this out on our own.

This can lead us to exit our moratorium having achieved unhealthy money beliefs—and then this is our moneyself, unless or until we change it.

Bonus Stage: Middlescence: The Renegotiation

Gerontologist Barbara Waxman, author of *The Middlescence Manifesto*, says that if we live long enough and are lucky, we go through a second adolescence—middlescence. Just like adolescence, our bodies are teeming with hormones as they change; we straddle between not being young anymore and not being old; we try on new identities, experiment with possibilities, and reexamine and question much of life, what we've been told, and what we believe. Middlescence is a stage, not an age, although chronologically it's said to happen between the ages of 45-65 (some people earlier, some later).

Middlescence is not the midlife crisis society would lead us to believe it is, although unsettling at times. Instead, it's an opportunity to reset the factory settings. Absolutely everything is up for renegotiation: work, lifestyle, money, (all) relationships, health, and establishing new boundaries in each of these areas. We accept ourselves (finally!) as who we are and act accordingly. We rediscover, dust off the young parts, and put them to great purpose.

We ask big questions like teenagers do:

- Who am I (now)?
- Who do I want to be?
- What do I want to do?
- Learn?
- How do I want to spend my time and money?
- What will be different in the future?

Based on my experience with clients, middlescence presents a gauntlet of facing fears, stretching beyond capabilities to live into our potential, and, the absolute hardest part, facing up to our past by allowing ourselves to dive deep and feel all the feels of a very painful or disappointing history—to heal moments of disassociation and self-protection coping mechanisms in money matters.

A big shift in perspective about time occurs—it moves faster. We spend less time looking back, are more present and future-focused. It's the stage where we have the experience, capacity, and drive to make the most of everything, savor relationships, money, energy, and time, and contribute to the world. It's a time where we can cast off those shackles that previously bound us in our thinking and our actions and choose to do the things we always wanted to. Middlescence is our beautiful combination of leveraging our sense of fun and our wisdom, and choosing to make peace with the past while building an even greater future.

This stage—this state of mind, really—melds youthful exuberance and accrued wisdom, while fostering reconciliation with the past and the construction of a brighter future. A second opportunity materializes: a chance to bridge the gap and fully tap into your financial capabilities.

Let me add my voice to the choir and encourage you to embrace this stage. You possess more capital—both emotional and experiential—than at any previous time in your life. Today is the youngest you'll ever be again, and it's the perfect time to reevaluate and ask yourself: "What do I want to major in for the rest of my life?" With the depth of knowledge and life experiences you have, you're being called—perhaps even dared—to approach finance differently, to chase after your desires, and to heed your calling.

Become the financial success the Universe intends you to be. Trust in yourself; your potential for greatness is real, and now, you can manifest prosperity in ways you once only dreamt of.

Next

As you can see, our earliest memories of money and how the adult role models in our lives behaved around it absolutely shape our financial identities. For better or for worse (and usually it's for worse), these subconscious patterns are captaining the ship of our money lives.

Changing them, however, is not hard. It's rather straightforward, actually. It takes some moxie and mojo and some time reflecting and journaling. If you've related to any of the feelings or stories shared so far, you've already started the process.

It is important for you to examine and reflect on not just your moneyisms and flashpoints, but how they consolidate into your identity—your moneyself—so that we can continue to dive even deeper and, ultimately, script your future and own your money narrative. This is powerful work on the things you can and must change to reach your full financial potential. These prompts will get you where you want to go.

Moneyself Exercises

It's time to acknowledge and validate your current money-self and lay the foundation for the house your future self will live in. In the next journal prompts, be generous with your grace and self-talk, be bold in your dreams, and be unflinching in your resolve to create the future you want.

1. How are any dormant, unexamined money beliefs from your past calling the shots in your wallet today? How does that play out in your financial behavior?

2. Which stage of money identity formation do you think you're in—childhood, adolescence, later adolescence, adulthood, or middlescence? Are there elements of your financial identity that you'd like to challenge and/or grow-up?

3. Think of "middlescence" as a glorious reboot in the middle of your life. It's a second debut, only this time you're armed with experience and wisdom. Consider your present financial status and objectives. How has your perception of money and your financial identity evolved over time, particularly during significant life phases like mid-life?

4. How can you make peace with your financial past? No guilt trips. No shoulding. What's done is done, and the beauty is you get a second act. What will you do differently? What old bridges can you mend or new ones can you build to realize your full financial potential? Write it *all* down. Whether it's saving more, investing wisely, or just cutting yourself some slack and acknowledging your progress—put it on paper.

7

The Duality of Money—How to Allow What We Want

*E*veryone I've ever met, whether personally or professionally, shares a universal goal, or rather a desire, to have all the money they will ever need to support their lifestyle. In other words, we all want to be financially free. We are chasing after the feelings that come with reaching our goals—feelings that money alone cannot buy, like satisfaction, energy, comfort, fun, joy, peace, excitement, gratitude, feeling needed, and feeling cared for. There's often a disconnect in setting emotional goals and actually pursuing these goals through financial means to unlock these benefits. All this emotional possibility exists as long as we are thoughtful in our pursuits.

Using Money Situationally

Based on what I've seen in more than 25 years as a financial advisor and confidant, the poverty of prosperity usually comes from using our money situationally. Using money situationally is when we change our financial behavior based on circumstances and emotional motiva-tions. In other words, we act like financial chameleons.

For example, while we may manage money objectively and strategically at work, we don't always do so in our personal lives. Maybe this involves neglecting your personal budget, while you are perfectly capable of managing a billion-dollar budget for your company. Or perhaps you want peace and harmony at home with your spouse, so you avoid any and all money conversations—yet at the office, you can easily negotiate your salary with your manager.

It's easy to focus on the poverty part of the poverty of prosperity. We worry that we aren't good enough, or that there's something wrong with us. But let's remember that *most* of our life exists in prosperity. We have high incomes, good success, often good jobs, and often good relationships. The real problem isn't that we don't have the financial knowledge. The real problem is that the skills in these areas aren't transferring to our relationship with money.

My crazy stories aside, lots of people struggle to make ends meet despite earning a high income. They haven't mastered the difference between earning a living, afford-ability, or income versus wealth, whether they are buying a car instead of groceries or cashing out the 401(k) to cover out-of-control bills.

Donna

SO MANY OF us are in this situation, and yet we all feel alone. As we look around us, we may think that everyone else has it figured out. We often think *Hey, if she's a power-house at work, she must be the same at home.*

My client Donna knows this isn't the case. At the office, Donna has exactly the money relationship that she wants.

She's at the top of her game, well compensated, knows the value she delivers, and owns the contribution she makes. She is unapologetic about quoting fees, handles negotiations and difficult conversations masterfully, and exudes confidence. She's clear about what she wants and has given herself permission to advocate for her money.

The problem is—she's the complete opposite at home. There is such a disparity between her money relationship with her clients and with her money relationship with her husband, that she's unrecognizable to herself. As a result, she feels like a hypocrite. Donna's husband controls all of the household money.

When they married young, they agreed that he would be in charge. As she's grown and has become a successful businesswoman, she realizes that she and her husband need to share the financial burden and control, but she struggles to explain this to him. She feels derailed because she doubts herself and her abilities to communicate and be an equal partner in financial decisions at home.

Donna feels like an imposter because she doesn't conduct herself at home with the same level of personal power as she does with her clients. She's admitted to feeling ashamed and fearful that her clients would fire her on the spot "if they only knew."

Fear of being found out is terrifying, especially if we feel hopeless to change our situation. Donna felt powerless to act.

But after doing the work in chapter 5, Donna realized that she had foreclosed on the belief from her childhood that "Money is private." This belief was why she avoided money conversations with her husband and what led to her ceding control to him early on in their marriage. It set the tone and the roles each of them have played in the years that followed, and those "factory settings" were never revisited again to reflect the natural changes that occur over a time span of several decades.

Suddenly it all made sense why everything was so "off" about her money at home.

Donna's situational approach to money stemmed from cognitive dissonance, caused by her conflicting beliefs: in the office, she believed that money is *not* private and found that talking about it fosters trust and teamwork. In contrast, at home, she held the opposite belief that money *is* private, leading her to avoid financial discussions. This clash between her work and home beliefs caused psychological discomfort.

Once she understood the discrepancy between her opposing beliefs, she stopped waiting for permission and stood in her power with the same clarity she leverages as the boss at the office, and now uses those skills at home, too. She now negotiates and speaks up in conversations that she used to avoid because she sees herself differently and recognizes all the valuable skills she brings to the table.

Donna still counts on her husband, but she now does so as a team player rather than a follower. Her story exemplifies what happens to a lot of us who get stuck in an unchecked, old pattern. It also exemplified what is possible for all of us: updating our beliefs and choices to realize our full financial potential. As a result, Donna and her husband are living their happily ever after.

The Duality of Money

When it comes to people's relationships with money, things can appear to be one way when, in reality, they are another. Consider my parents. They were very successful people. They lived in a good neighborhood, had a thriving business, cared about how we did in school, and had a large and vibrant group of friends. In fact, you might say they were a power couple, and on one hand that was true. They were just *not* powerful with money.

But they could have been—and that's the part that hurts. It's probably hurting you, too, if you have a strong desire to uplevel where you are but aren't even sure why you can't seem to get it together.

My parents are not alone. As touched on in chapter one, the real problem is the poverty of prosperity, or the making of money but not keeping it, and it affects more people than you may think. You might have read a headline at some point about a professional athlete who lived the rich-and-famous lifestyle and then ended up with nothing when their career was over.

What doesn't make the headlines as much are sobering statistics like these:

- 41 percent of Americans earning over $200,000 a year have cried over not having enough money.
- One-third of Americans report difficulty in covering basic expenses, and that includes 16 percent of people making between $100 thousand and $199 thousand, and 8 percent who earn over $200 thousand.
- As many as 63 percent of Americans get by with loans from their families. More than one-third of friends loan one another money, as do one in six coworkers.
- 50 percent of adult Americans have no retirement savings at all.

These statistics reflect symptoms of the deeper problem

of poverty of prosperity. Maybe this sounds like you. If it does, you're not alone.

Are You Living with the Poverty of Prosperity? Lots of People Are.

The Poverty of Prosperity has layers and stages to it. It can look a lot of different ways:

- Someone who is completely out of control with their personal finances, but still crushes it at work
- People who have success optics, but are scarcely making ends meet and know they could be (or need to be) doing more
- Someone who has more than enough, yet is avoidant, uncomfortable, and lives in fear about their financial future

In every case, these people do not *feel* wealthy. In fact, they feel uncomfortable navigating their financial status and assets. They barely acknowledge their discomfort and hide their feelings.

This internal conflict and reluctance to face their true financial emotions can often be traced back to deeper underlying issues in their approach to life's objectives. There are three missing links from the goal setting process that provide insight into these challenges: (1) wanting more and the "anti-goal," (2) self-permission, and (3) a clear definition of the endgame.

Wanting More and the Anti-Goal

There is a conversation within the financial planning community right now about how most clients don't really know what their goals are. They are clear that they want to set goals; they just don't know how to translate their dreams, aspirations, and goals into numbers. When they meet with their financial advisor, they often describe what they want emotionally and qualitatively, saying things like, "I just want to get to the place where I have choices," or "I just want to know where I am and where I'm going." Setting and striving to reach goals is an undeniable part of the human experience, but it takes *many* conversations to get to the core of what somebody truly wants their money to provide for them, and the people and values they hold closest.

Our desires and direction always point to receiving more in life and getting more out of life. It's the process of becoming more of who we are that brings us to our next levels of being. This, in turn, directs us toward fulfilling our soul's purpose and receiving the worldly possessions that we desire as a result.

After we give ourselves permission to accumulate wealth and strive for our goals, we must clearly define our goals, and, almost more importantly, our "anti-goal." Our anti-goal, the thing we *don't* want to happen, is often far easier to identify than our actual goal.

Humans feel the pain of loss twice as much as the pleasure of gain. It only makes sense, then, that we talk about "anti-goals" or consider the negative outcomes we want to avoid in the future. We may want to avoid a past mistake or a lived experience or look at someone as an anti-mentor who models what not to do, for example. This "anti-goal" can be conceived in many ways.

On a psychological level, we all have fears over future regret. We don't want to look back on our lives and wish we had taken more chances with our careers or our money. Perhaps you don't want to regret not taking more time off to be with family or giving more to those in need when you could have afforded to donate. Or you worry that you won't be able to write a check in full and send the kids to college debt-free while balancing your own needs. Perhaps you want to live more for today because your father passed away too young and never got to enjoy the fruits of his labor. Maybe you want to make sure you retire "on time" so you can enjoy it because you've seen too many retire and then die shortly thereafter. We need to spray paint bright red lines in the sand about what we don't want.

Mine was clear and simple: don't be like my parents with money. That was a start, but it wouldn't be enough to get me where I wanted to go. I'd also need to translate that anti-goal to the affirmative, and add actual numbers. Finding this type of crystal clear clarity cannot be crowd-sourced.

Few people I've met have expressed their goals in literal terms, such as wanting to "beat the markets," without an express reason or purpose for wanting the money. Money is too personal to let markets define our goals for us or to relate our achievements to only the balances of our account values or market performance (or underperformance). Money is a front-of-mind aspiration that we relate with through our definition of *la dolce vita*.

Goal setting is a winding process that requires us to go from broad brushstrokes to fine details. Most goal setting in the financial planning process is clinical. It centers on gathering data (facts, figures), financial analysis, and developing a plan and set of actions. And then, late in the game, there comes a conversation about compromises in order to get results. Advisors will begin to adjust inflation or portfolio rates of return and ask clients whether they are willing to retire later, save more, work part-time, fund less for college, take fewer vacations, etc.

Self-Permission

Every journey starts with glimmers of hope about the future. We're always dreaming of future versions of ourselves and what life will be like. When it feels tangible, like a reality we can manifest, and we are confident in our abilities to act, research shows we have high "self-efficacy." Positive self-efficacy beliefs are known to be highly correlated with goal attainment. However, before we can truly have self-efficacy, we need to first engage in self-permission.

Self-permission is the ultimate negotiation because it happens within. It's the power play that allows us to embrace our passions, with or without the approval of others. Also, it allows us to act because we're giving ourselves consent to behave and feel a certain way to acquire what we want. There's always a moment when we must ask ourselves, "Am I allowed to do this?" and if we answer in the affirmative, we are ready to move forward.

Defining the End Game

This brings me to the misnomer that many people have that it's a financial advisor's job to tell you what's affordable. Noooooo. First of all, affordability and possibility are not the same thing. Affordability has the potential to cancel possibility out. Who wants fewer possibilities? Not you. Otherwise, you wouldn't be reading this book.

It's not an advisor's (or anyone else's) job to tell you what is possible for your life. Their job is to listen closely to what you want, why you want it, and to support you in getting it. The great news about building wealth is that just about everyone is self-made. Most of us only ever inherit family values, attitudes, and mindsets. Get rich quick schemes are a sham. Very few people win the lottery or inherit life-changing amounts of money. Consider people with wealth and abundance, and assume that nearly everyone has been or is in the same boat as you in that they worked to translate their income into wealth.

An advisor's job is not to tell you what to do with your one and only life. They are there to help you consider the tradeoffs, sacrifices, and commitments you are and aren't willing to make, and to help you make and stick to your plans. When you outgrow your plan (and you will), it's their job to help you to make another. Let's put it out there and both agree that most of what you really want in life requires money. The proof that you can make it financially is all around you.

You need to clearly define what that specifically looks like to you. One yacht or two. Chandeliers or candles. Bike or jet. Artisan French truffles or mega-chain candy bars. Whatever!

Money Duality Exercises

Money can be tricky, but it doesn't have to be. Below, we'll explore the duality of money, and how to allow in more of what you want in your financial life.

1. Identify two financial areas where you act "situationally." What emotions or thoughts tend to accompany these events? Are there any common triggers or patterns that you've noticed when it comes to these situations?
2. Where are you "crushing it?" What might you "borrow" (skills, knowledge, attitude, outlook) from another area of life and apply to your finances?
3. What are you not allowing or impeding your own abundance? What kind of self-permission do you need to grant yourself to achieve, become, or realize your full financial potential?
4. What are your specific financial goals? As important, what are the "anti-goals" (negative outcomes) you want to avoid in the future?
5. What's your financial endgame? What dreams do you have for your life?

8

Command Your New Money Relationship

*W*hen people are anxious about money, or want to find a financial edge, they often look outside of themselves for easy answers. But the answers are not outside of you—rather, they are inside, lurking in memories, secrets, and patterns you may not even realize you have. Exploring and uncovering your own idiosyncrasies through the theories and ideas we discussed in chapters 2-7 are essential to you commanding a better relationship with money. And you deserve it.

The path to feeling more secure with money, with a net worth to match, is the path to realizing your full financial potential. Security, prosperity, and purpose aren't found in one perfect calculation that will take away all your money worries (and they aren't found in more budgeting, saving, or investing information). They come from converting new insights about yourself into inspired action.

To catapult your financial trajectory and reach your full financial potential, you need to analyze and leverage the six key components that got you to where you are financially: your flashpoints, moneyisms, secrecy bias, moneyself, emotional drivers, and your money scripts. Then, you need to look at where there are opportunities to get in more balance, so that you can command a better relationship with money. That means doing more of what you already know how to do, and integrating the transferable skills you've already developed into your relationship with money.

Money Scripts Aren't Your Destiny, They're Your Diagnostic

Your moneyhood: flashpoints, moneyisms, secrecy bias, moneyself, emotional drivers, and money scripts are not your destiny—they're your diagnostic. They are a snapshot in time that is totally changeable—if you want and if you put in the work.

Given that most people are operating against their best interests because of outdated beliefs, and that you are reading the words on this page right now, I'm guessing you're up for an upgrade.

Acknowledge Competing Commitments

For example, if you follow the money avoidant script and avoid thinking or talking about money, you'll likely be at odds with yourself when you try to implement a budget. In other words, you'll have competing commitments, such as simultaneously being dedicated to following a budget, while also being utterly avoidant of tracking your expenses or balancing your bank account.

After attending my workshop, "How Many Manolos Does It Take to Retire?" one of my best clients referred a friend to me—Angela. Angela has a gazillion pairs of shoes but wants to buy a co-op and retire in New York City. She will not call because she is sure that I am the shoe police and will tell her to cease and desist buying all kicks. Talk about a competing commitment. In her head, it's an either/or. In my head, it's a "yes, and." I want Angela—and everyone—to have their shoes and wear them, too. Proportions matter, though.

What I think is sort of funny (and sad) is that this lady knows little about me, especially how much I love fashion and relate to her highly.

My antenna is up, sensing that shoes are freedom. Or rather that choosing to buy shoes is an act of freedom for this woman. She doesn't need me to join the chorus of her inner bossypants already in her ear, telling her to stop buying shoes. But she doesn't know that I *get* that.

Her resistance tells me she's wrestling with the "ought to" and "want to" sides within. It also indicates that she doesn't want to compound the internal pressure she feels to do better by adding external pressure from a person like me—or at least the character she perceives me to be.

Shoes may represent an act of rebellion, and a means to alleviate her self-imposed pressure. In all likelihood, she gets some temporary relief with every new pair she buys, and never reconciles the actual conflict between wanting both financial preparedness and feeling free.

My educated guess is that she has internalized other people's socially acceptable idea(s) of what being set for life means and associates discipline, restraint, and self-control as the only methods of getting there. There are two issues at hand: (1) she hasn't defined what set for life means to *her* and (2) hasn't actually calculated the true value of the trade-offs she is and is not willing to make to get to her financial destination. Until she examines what's really going on, she will continue to feel controlled and will seek to balance that out with the freedom she feels walking in those high heels of hers.

She knows that she needs—and actually wants: a financial collaborator, yet also wants to keep buying shoes even if it means avoiding her long-term plans. If she doesn't overcome her avoidance and inability to talk through her situation, she will stunt her financial growth and hinder her financial potential.

Competing Commitments

Every financial situation creates competing commitments. Yet it's likely that you are not even aware of the conflict within yourself that simultaneously pushes and pulls. These dual needs compromise decision-making and diminish follow-through as your mind struggles to choose between two things that you want at the same time. There's nothing wrong with this; in fact, it's natural and happens all the time to all of us.

The resistance you feel is like an indicator light on a car's mechanical panel. This feeling is a tool that can help you identify your belief systems and your competing commitments. It's like a check engine light.

If you find yourself shaming yourself about your money, I want you to stand up and do five jumping jacks right now. For real—right now. If you are cozied up, fair enough, just move your arms. Why are we doing jumping jacks in the middle of a finance book? I want to interrupt your pattern, so you stop the shaming and get on with the noticing.

Instead of name calling, bullying, and shoulding (unproductive), I want you observing, accepting, and strategizing (building your self-knowledge and conscious choices).

It is important that we aren't afraid of information that helps us understand ourselves better. Self-knowledge leads to growth. Besides, our current beliefs are not our destiny. The inventory of our current beliefs is a personal roadmap that highlights areas for introspection and growth.

Once we know what our beliefs are, we have a new seat at the table—we're in a new position of power. With this knowledge, we can begin the process of transformation.

Neuroplasticity: The Clue to Up-Leveling Our Financial Potential

The clue to changing our story, and therefore, our financial potential, is embedded in what we discussed earlier: how your beliefs were formed in the first place. Don't worry, this does not require a mix tape, three cans of hairspray, going to the mall, negotiating curfew, or any other teenage drama.

Instead, we want to mimic stage four of the belief formation process of your moneyself: moratorium. This is the critical examination stage, where we try on different behaviors. In the present time, we bring your beliefs back into your conscious mind for examination. This will also tie into your results and findings from the money scripts quiz, where you learned your primary set of (subconscious) money beliefs.

Now it's time to decide: are these beliefs serving you?

If they aren't, then you can begin to leverage the magic of middlescence, upgrade your factory settings on financial beliefs, renegotiate the game plan, and intentionally choose new thoughts. When you go to check the budget and feel avoidant, you can tell yourself that it's savvy to be fully aware of your financial situation. This will resolve the competing commitment in your mind and allow you to dig into the numbers.

One way to find new thoughts that are likely to resolve your competing commitments is to consider the items with which you agreed on the money script assessment and then flip them. For example, if you "agreed" with the statement "I don't deserve money," which is a money avoidant thought, then it would be helpful to work to acquire the new thought: "I deserve money." As you learn more about the less helpful beliefs that are driving your behavior, you will be able to consciously change them by changing your thoughts.

This is because new thoughts, once you've conditioned yourself to have them enough times, will eventually solidify into new beliefs. These new beliefs will motivate new behaviors, which will intrinsically lead to new, healthier *unconscious* habits (the gold standard of beliefs impacting actions). Ultimately, this is how you change your beliefs to change your life.

The Brain Is a Belief-Creating Machine

If this sounds too simple, then you are not giving enough credit to your brain—it's a belief-creating machine. The brain is quick to pick up new beliefs, once you prove that you do, in fact, believe them. The process of consciously choosing and focusing on new thoughts will trigger your brain's natural state: neuroplasticity.

Neuroplasticity is the term used to describe how your brain changes over time. Scientifically, it's the ability for our neural circuits to make adaptive changes on both a structural and functional level.

Before modern research, it was believed that the brain didn't change much past adolescence. Now we know that our brain continues to evolve all throughout our life, all the way through old age. When our brain changes, it carves new paths, and each time we have a new thought, it strengthens that thought by deepening the neural pathway and making this thought more likely to occur again in the future.

Choose a Believable Belief

Christine once believed that "All highly educated people are smart and rich." She truly believed that a person had to be really smart, like, MENSA-level intelligence, to get ahead. She picked this up somewhere along the way in childhood—not sure from who, what, or where exactly. And for her, it was a limiting belief. She did not see herself as one of these "smart" people who could accumulate wealth.

Then Christine started noticing people in her workplace with high school and average college educations doing quite well financially due to smarts as well as hard work, access, and luck.

She went from an ivory tower type of thinking to one influenced by her own observations in the real world. Her coworkers led her to realize how much human capital is involved in one's success: what you know, who you know, and who you're being.

It was an observation that led to a revelation and ultimately, she focused on cultivating relationships more than she ever had before. And when she connected others and got connected herself, she was able to build a career safety net. She realized her colleagues had the same resources that she also had. Although some had Ivy League educations, most did not. Christine watched what they did and how they did it. She came to believe, "I can

have what they have and can do what they're doing
—better."

When we want to change a belief, it's often hard to go
from black to white. Therefore, we need to choose a new,
believable belief. We need to choose the next best thing we
can believe about a situation to move us in the direction in
which we want to go.

Then, when this new thought is activated or used more
frequently, it will ultimately overtake an "old" thought. As
the "old" thought becomes the "path less traveled,"
(because it's pushed aside by the new thought), it weakens,
and the neural pathway decays. Eventually, the new
thought dominates, and you gain a new, more helpful
belief. This is neuroplasticity.

As an example, consider these two thoughts:

Old thought: "It's too scary to look at my money."

New thought: "It's smart to understand and manage
my finances."

To be clear, the new thought has to work for you. If
you don't think being money savvy is all that important,
then this isn't the new thought for you. Instead, you might
choose "Caring about money doesn't make me a bad
person." Ideally, however, it's best that you choose a statement in the affirmative, such as, "Caring about money is
the responsible thing to do for my present and future."

The goal is to feel good about the new thought, as this
will prompt you to nurture and focus on it more often. It'll
also encourage your brain to make that thought automatic
as quickly as possible.

In the beginning, you will need to build your awareness
of the old thought coming up. You will have to stop, recognize it, have a pep talk, and choose the new thought. It
sometimes helps to have a written note on your phone or a
Post-it note in your wallet, that you read and repeat to

yourself when you are trying to redirect your thoughts. As you do this, you are not only reinforcing your new thought, you are starving your old thought of the strength it once held.

Eventually, as you force yourself to think about how savvy you are again and again, you will strengthen that new thought enough that it will begin to occur naturally—like a belief. This is because the neurons that fire the new thought have become more robust. Your brain really likes to fire familiar thoughts, which means it won't be long before your new thought is your new belief. Soon, your new unconscious habit will form, and you'll be checking your budget every day.

This process shows us that we are always capable of changing our mindset by introducing new thoughts. I don't want to make it sound easy, but I want you to understand that it's actually a very natural, normal, matter-of-fact process. Your brain is designed to create new beliefs—why not choose them consciously and support it through the transition with self-talk?

Works for Everything

Great news: you can leverage your brain's beautiful neuro-plasticity for *any belief.* In the next four chapters, we're going to examine the most powerful, granddaddy belief of them all, the one that keeps you struggling, the one that traps you in a deathloop of competing commitments, the one that keeps you anxious and insecure.

It's the belief that, when changed, will heal your struggle with money, resolve your competing commitments, and help you create wealth and financial security.

That changeable belief is: talking about money is bad. It's not. In fact, talking about money is critical to our financial well-being—even though we often believe that it should require the highest level of national security clearance to discuss because it's so secret and precarious—the opposite is true. And that truth will set you free—financially free. You can learn how to have productive conversations about money so you can reach your full financial potential.

Too Much Too Soon

Accepting the truth about our financial habits and beliefs and taking action to change them are steps many aren't prepared to take. Facing our money stories demands not just courage, but also an open heart and mind. Based on behavioral change models, research indicates that only 20% of people who recognize the need for change are actually ready to take action and make those changes in their lives. This is a story about someone who wasn't yet ready to change.

Jocelyne was a fifty-five-year-old C-suite executive earning an annual salary of $1.1 million. She's a good example of someone who has been successful in life: climbed the corporate ladder, served as a leader in her community, and was a devoted wife and mother. However, she had nothing saved for her future and was on the brink of financial failure.

Jocelyne didn't fear the possibility of financial ruin; her fear was much deeper than that. *She feared being seen.* Her secret wasn't only that she was nearly insolvent. It was that she wasn't living the life that she wanted. Deep down, she wished that she had made her living as a novelist and tried making up for her career dissatisfaction by spending as a means to heal her broken spirit. She believed that "more money would fix" all of her problems when what she really needed was to rearrange her relationship with money and time.

In my eyes, Jocelyne had everything it took to change her relationship with money from ho-hum to hot damn. The only problem was she didn't believe in herself as much as I did.

Revealing too much too soon, our conversations flew too close to the sun and she ended up ghosting me. Why? Because it's not that talking about money is hard—it's talking about our *feelings* about money that is hard. People have to be ready to accept the truth about their money beliefs and behaviors in order to change. It's too painful for some—the risk of being seen and rejected for who we really are strikes at the heart of our identity and stirs up our deepest fears of not being loved and accepted. Professionally speaking, Jocelyne will always be the "one that got away"—she just wasn't ready.

Better Than Therapy

Changing your relationship with money means healing your money story. Healing your money story means finding your voice.

I'm not suggesting you drop everything and run to your rooftop, nudge your way to a red dot on a TEDx stage, or plan a social takeover. We have more important lessons to cover first. But I want you to know that it's where we're going. Doing the exercises presented thus far will undoubtedly move the needle on improving your financial trajectory and reaching your full potential. No doubt. But I don't want you to stop there. I urge you to keep going because the real game-changer—the holy grail of your financial future—is yet to come. These first chapters were the warm-up. The radical, light-up-your-life, don't-miss-this-step is talking about money—out loud—to another human.

I'm suggesting you go public in private, *public in private*, with the right people to talk about the things that really matter.

You've listened to the gurus, read the books, taken the classes, searched the internet for answers, and yet, nothing has broken you through to the level you seek.

Talking about money will. If you are willing to try this "radical" idea, I know that you will experience an earth-shattering transformation. Even if talking about money only relieved our stress, we would be way ahead because, boy, are we stressed about money. The American Psychological Association has reported finances as a top life stressor; around 67% of us are stressed about it.

We all know what it's like to face an unexpected financial event. Imagine receiving an unbudgeted tax bill in the mail that you don't have the funds for. If you really imagine this scenario, you may experience a visceral response: maybe you feel your heart drop to your stomach, or reach for a bag of double chocolate Milano cookies. Perhaps you think about packing your bags, taking off in your car, and driving to an undisclosed location without leaving a forwarding address—or even selling your car altogether.

This is your fear instinct ("fight or flight") kicking in— the panic, the doomsday thoughts, the immediate move to thinking about "quick" fixes that are (usually) terrible ideas. Psychologists call this a "scarcity mindset." According to several studies, our brains act differently when we perceive or anticipate scarcity. Specifically, people get dumber. For real! One study found that when subjects simply *thought* about a big bill that would strain their finances, their cognitive abilities plummeted by an average of 14 IQ points—a similar deficit to pulling an all-nighter.

Obviously, ignoring your money stress is nothing but bad news. Eating your favorite cookies or taking a drive may make you feel better in the moment, but it's not a long-term solution. Neither is selling your car, unless you have a fleet of them. Learning how to open up and talk about money is more than just a way of sharing information. It's a way of sorting and figuring out complex and emotional money decisions.

Money conversations done well can trigger positive physical and emotional changes in the brain that can open you up to having productive and trusting dialog that allows you to be seen, understood, and helped. This, all by itself, without any extra advice or insight, can make you feel much, much better.

I've been a financial advisor for decades, and countless clients have told me that our conversations are "better than therapy." Hearing that has become my professional hallmark. To know that they feel comfortable enough to share their money stories, often for the first time, without shame or judgment, means as much to them as it does to me. One thing I hear time and again is what a relief it is to learn that they are not alone. Knowing that often loosens up a lot of anxiety and makes it easier to build new habits. And it's not just talking to me that makes a difference.

More than one couple has told me that their conversations with each other have improved, leading to a great reduction in stress. One woman told me that she and her husband's newfound ability to talk about money has made their partnership stronger, and her husband doesn't worry about money the way he did when he felt wholly responsible for every financial decision.

Finally, when people start talking about money, their own mind and mindset changes. Most people carry some unhealthy beliefs about money around with them. Clients routinely tell me that they are able to upgrade their money story and adopt healthier beliefs just by talking it out. One client had stayed at an unsatisfying job for years based on the belief that she was lucky to have just enough. When she shifted her belief to "I want more," she was suddenly motivated to find a new job and got one that was much more of a fit.

Another client came to me fully entrenched in avoiding money discussions, carrying the belief that you simply can't get everything you want. When she shifted to the belief that "Being money conscious is how you get everything you want," she was able to strategize about money with new and game-changing vigor.

The Importance of Talking about Money

In order to heal your relationship with money, you need to find your voice and start talking about it. Finding your voice has several aspects—there's how you talk to yourself (self-talk), identifying the old beliefs that don't serve you, choosing new beliefs, and creating and conditioning your new moneyself.

Talking about money—and admitting your idiosyncrasies and conflicting commitments—is hard. This territory can bring the imposter feeling—it can lend to a nagging, hypercritical voice that tells you you're failing; and you may worry that you're ruining your financial future. Whatever your financial situation, whatever your strengths and worries, keeping these worries in the dark is a dangerous, money-sucking proposition.

So let's do the opposite. You deserve a strong, thriving, best-it-can-be financial trajectory. The way there is to write and talk your way through the steps in this book. I know how hard it can be—I kept the yacht debacle a secret for more than 30 years. At the same time, though, I fed my obsession with financial psychology and moved my way up in my career to a partner at a top financial advisory firm. This book exists to live my life's purpose of helping as many people as possible find their way through the financial forest.

After these next exercises to help you command a better relationship with money, the next four chapters will share even more tools to catapult yourself upward and forward so you can be your best moneyself, living your best and fullest financial potential. All you have to do is say yes.

Money Command Exercises

Below are the tasks necessary to help you make the transition to command your new money relationship.

1. From chapter 5, which belief did you pick to change? Write down the old belief, and label it as "old belief."
2. Is this belief tied up in a financial flashpoint, a moneyism, a habit of self-sabotage, or perhaps shrouded in secrecy? Maybe it's linked to how you emotionally relate to money or the scripts you've been rehearsing all your life? Describe the context around the belief you are choosing to change.
3. How does this belief hold you back? What is this belief costing you financially, emotionally, relationship-wise, health-wise, and knowledge-wise?
4. On a scale from 1 to 7, (7 being 100% ready) how ready are you to rewrite your future financial life?
5. Challenge yourself by writing down the opposite belief. Then a belief that's midway. Then one that's believable, if either of these is not yet. Now edit that statement to one that excites you. Flip it, twist it, tear it apart, and name it—write your new belief in a way that will catalyze your growth.
6. My new belief is:

   _____.

7. How are you going to keep this shiny new belief front and center? Post-it notes on your mirror? In your wallet, like me? A daily mantra?

Reminder alarm? Journal? Incorporate into a daily task?

8. With your new belief in mind, what or how will you act differently? What clues will you need to see to believe you're changing?

9. How often will you look for proof this new belief is taking root? Multiple times daily (recommended), daily, weekly, monthly?

Go on, don't just read this—act on it. This isn't a dress rehearsal. The next scene's all yours.

9

Self-Talk—The Invisible Force

*O*ne of my dearest friends, Grace, is an inspiring example of how transformative it can be to open up and discuss your financial situation candidly. After her divorce, Grace relied on her financial settlement to make ends meet and to reinvent herself as a solopreneur. Without her knowing it at the time, taxes weren't taken from the withdrawals she took. This landed her in a complicated situation where she couldn't pay what she owed the IRS.

Grace avoided filing tax returns. She was stuck in a negative thought loop about what to do: get a job or pursue her entrepreneurial dreams. She worried her tax status would make her unhirable. And if she landed a job, she thought she would lose the independence she valued or the alignment with her soul's purpose. These worries kept her mind going around and around in circles.

Despite working with a job coach and being runner up for several positions, she hadn't landed a job. Nor was she any closer to realizing the full income potential in her business. Grace stayed stuck for eight long and arduous years.

Out of frustration, she started reading books (like this one) on money mindset, financial therapy, and behavioral economics. She began to wonder if the opposite of some of her thoughts might be true. For example, her inner voice said things like: "Other people deserve money," but "You'll always only ever just scrape by." At first, she simply allowed herself to notice these thoughts, and then question them.

Before long, she started to imagine what it would be like to feel like she did deserve money. She wondered what life would be like if she had *more* than what she needed. The power of thinking of new possibilities opened her up to the idea of dealing with her taxes. For the first time, she was willing to discuss her taxes and ask for help.

Grace's decision to hire an accountant changed everything. He immediately cut through the noise in her head and looked at her situation strictly by the numbers. It's no surprise that he advised her on several solutions—finding money from the government that she could use to defray past taxes, penalties, and the interest that she owed, as well as the best corporate structure for her business. She marveled that the very first meeting with her new accountant literally brought money in!

Resolving her tax situation was easier than she imagined. She got on a payment plan, cleared up what she owed, and told me that *the moment* she made the appointment to speak with an accountant, a slew of new business came in. For the first time, she felt like an established, bona fide businessperson.

Talking about her financial situation allowed Grace to get the outside perspective and expertise that she needed to move forward with confidence. She wondered why she had put it off for so long. Once she let her secret out, she felt released from the mental and emotional burden she'd been carrying. And, if you can believe it, she says she's "excited to pay quarterly taxes."

Invisible Force out in the Wild

Knowing what your money scripts and beliefs are won't do much good unless you're able to call them out in the wild. And a perfect place to start to learn how to recognize the "invisible force" within is to listen to how you talk to yourself about money.

How most people talk to themselves about money is not fun. Why? Because we talk to ourselves like total jerkholes.

It's easier and more productive to talk about money with other people if you know how to properly talk to yourself about it, so we have to start with ourselves. Even though most of us have been told that talking about money is private, we can choose to change this and learn to have better conversations inside our heads as well as out loud with other people.

Choose an Area of Focus

As we dive into self-talk, I want this chapter to feel tactically relevant and move you toward finding your voice. To do this, I would love for you to pick a topic you are struggling with or an area you'd like to improve, and consider your self-talk in light of that topic.

At the core of most money struggles is secrecy bias and avoidance of something: avoiding talking, avoiding facts, avoiding honest assessments. Secrecy bias and avoidance are linked, so it's not surprising that avoidance is a big feature.

Pick a common problem, which means something that touches directly on your concerns about money, and is very specific. I'm going to work through the example of *crazy busy overwhelm* as we progress through the steps.

The crazy busy overwhelm of life is an issue for many people. This issue can lead to an overload of commitments that lead to a cycle of perpetual busyness, struggling to regain control, only to be swept up by the demands of their schedule. This pattern slows people down from making better financial progress in their life.

Being overwhelmed with life has a way of making us feel stressed and forever behind, no matter how much money we make, and despite other great decisions like having a robust retirement account or lucrative investment properties.

Begin Within

All money conversations begin within. This means that to create a clean relationship with money, we must go in search of our self-talk. We also must be honest and curious enough about what we hear to challenge what comes up.

In chapter 4, we explored your moneyhood and identified where your deepest and most impactful money beliefs came from. I hope this eased some of the self-doubt and self-shaming that tends to permeate so many of our relationships with money. And yet, despite these insights, it can be challenging to speak to ourselves and about ourselves in a way that reflects the deep respect and empathy we deserve.

I've found that when it comes to money, people speak to themselves in ways they wouldn't ever dream of speaking to others. Nor would they tolerate anyone speaking to their loved ones in the ways in which they speak to themselves.

When it comes to overwhelm, in particular, I find that

people are very harsh. The sense of guilt they carry for not being able to allocate sufficient time and focus to make progress intensifies their frustration, causing people to engage in negative, shaming self-talk.

We need to change that.

Listen

The first step to breaking the habit of negative self-talk is realizing that you are doing it.

That can sound fairly obvious, causing you to wonder "Wouldn't I know if I was using negative self-talk?"

To this, I say, "Not necessarily."

Observe your thoughts over the next seven days and ask yourself:

- What do I hear?
- Where does the voice come from?
- Is the voice true?
- What am I getting out of listening to this voice?
- What do I want that I don't have?

IN MY PRACTICE, these are some of the common themes my clients have discovered over the last 25 years. Listen for your own self-talk, and write it down. You may be surprised what you come back to.

- I can't_____.
- It's too expensive.
- I don't have_____.
- Who do you think you are to … ask for a raise, to stay at the 5 star resort, to have money, to be

secure…?

- What's wrong with you? You should know (how to invest, how much to spend/save, how to stick to a budget/plan) and be good with money by now.
- You're so (fill in blank) … dumb, stupid, ditzy, lazy ….
- I'm lucky in love, not money.
- You can't have it all.
- It's too late, why even try?
- I can't afford to save, I'm just barely getting by.
- I wish someone would just take over for me.
- I have plenty of time. I'll figure all this out (later).
- Money will always be a struggle.

TIME and again I've heard insulting things that clients say out loud to themselves that they have no awareness of saying.

When I first met Bonnie, I heard her say, "I'm stupid with money" again and again. Bonnie is CEO of a family-owned business that, under her leadership, has tripled over the last few decades. She is smart and savvy. She has a law degree, for crying out loud! When I called her out on her comment, and we dove a little deeper, she shared that what she meant was that she didn't pay as much attention to her personal finances as she did to the company's. As a divorced mom with three children, work and family are her priorities, not her personal finances. After taking care of business and her children all day, the last thing Bonnie wants is to think about her money. She's too exhausted to.

I could have pretended not to hear the comment (I'm

stupid with money) and if I had, I would not have known what she really meant by it. It's easy to shortcut our language, but a lot healthier to speak a truth like "I'm crazy busy and I've been neglecting my personal money,"—that's an admission and an opportunity she and I have worked with.

Bonnie is not alone. I've witnessed clients saying a million disparaging things out loud about themselves when it comes to money:

I should know this.

I should be smarter.

I'm dumb as a rock when it comes to investing.

I'm clueless.

I'm so stupid.

I'm an idiot.

I don't have the time.

I'm a complete failure.

And other fill-in-the-blanks. Many people don't even realize they are saying these things out loud. When I call it out, we talk it out. I usually say something corny, like, "Stop talking about my friend Bonnie that way." In my experience, it's easier to talk about money and be receptive to the conversation when the mental block of thinking you're stupid or deficient is either challenged (nicely, of course) or out of the way.

This kind of self-talk is embedded in many of us, and is critical to uncover and expose to the sunlight so it can shrivel up and die a fast death.

Bonnie became aware of her own reference when I pointed it out to her. Only after she acknowledged it for the block it was, could we take steps toward making healthy changes.

We may tell ourselves that we are "only being honest." That we need a little "tough love," because we'll never find time (for example) if we don't address it head-on. And there's truth in that, so far as it goes. You can't go wrong by being honest with yourself and having the courage to address your problems directly. And, we can choose the brand of honesty that is kind, encouraging, and cheerleading. Not the brand of "honest" that is brutal, defeating, demoralizing and/or plain mean. You choose your brand. Who do you want to be?

There are two other truths I encourage you to consider as you think about how to manage your mind and heart during your quest to improve your relationship with money.

Truth #1: We Don't Thrive in Ongoing Stress

The human brain is designed to keep us alive. This means that when things get stressful, our brain begins to restrict our actions to safer, more predictable, reliable actions. We are more likely to fall back on old ways of being, shut down new skills, and become defensive.

If you find yourself berating yourself, or calling yourself names like "dumb-ass," "stupid," "idiot," or "screw-up," for running up your credit cards again, you are creating a high-pressure situation in your brain that is likely to keep you stuck. It's very challenging to be our best selves when we are stressed. This is because it takes a lot of courage to do things in new, healthy but unpredictable ways (that our brain simultaneously believes might kill us) when we already feel pressured and judged. Courage and resilience are limited resources under the best of times. We want to save it, if we can, for moments where we will need to be our best selves in conversation with others.

Truth #2: Harsh Self-Talk Is a Hiding Mechanism

People often use self-shame as a means of keeping painful truths hidden, even from themselves. If we worry that people may find out that we are a fraud (imposter syndrome), or that things are not how they seem, we will sometimes hype up how bad it would be if the truth came out. This can include exaggerated claims about negative reactions, and catastrophizing about consequences.

When we scare ourselves with exaggerated claims of negative consequences, we worry that people will reject us. Remember Andrew, who you met in chapter three, who was carrying a secret credit card that he hadn't told me about? When he came clean, he was sure I was going to stop working with him. And listen, we had to redo a lot of his plan, but I also understood. In the end, he hid his credit card from me to avoid having to deal with himself.

Avoiding and denying the truth of our money situation will allow the problem to grow, and prevent us from developing the kind of insight that will lead to positive change. And since this painful conversation is with yourself, there's no one to provide another point of view but you.

That view is the one that highlights your strengths, passions, skills, and other general badassery. If you're reading this book, you've probably done things that other people admire, like ran a marathon, attended every soccer game or school play your children participated in, or chaired an important fundraising event. These skills, passions, and strengths are available for you to use with money.

Bringing a more strengths-based approach to how you talk to yourself about your money struggles and lack of time will ensure that you don't forget how much you have to work with.

Third Person Talk

One fun way to accelerate the results of self-talk is to use third person self-talk. See, I've witnessed over and over and over again, that my clients who master how to talk to themselves with the kind, cheerleading, supportive brand of honesty and respect, have an easier time changing and talking about money at large.

One method of elevating our own internal dialog about money is by using distanced self-talk about money. This is defined as language that resembles how we talk to others, that we apply to how we talk to ourselves, according to Dr. Ethan Kross, a psychology professor at the University of Michigan. Basically, he means talking about ourselves in the third person. This talk-to-yourself-as-you-talk-to-others approach facilitates wise reasoning, instantly makes us feel better, and brings objectivity to the conversations we have in our heads. Just like talking to another person, using third person self-talk enhances the capacity to consider different viewpoints about ourselves. This makes talking about money easier.

One place to start is to consider your key message or belief that you'd like to adapt—one that will create new neural pathways that you want to nurture. Then, make it something believable for you, as well as something you'd like to hear / say / repeat. Use gorgeous and glorious language—or straight talk—or something in between if that's more your speed.

It's important to note that using third person self-talk is not the same as positive affirmations or a mantra, although the technique does use positive language. Rather, the use of third person pronouns (he, she, they) plus affirming language aims to create psychological distance from a problem or problem thinking, allowing us to assume thoughts and feelings as if they belong to someone else.

Getting back to Bonnie, she no longer says, "I'm stupid with money," to herself or out loud to me. Now she says:

"Bonnie does what she has to, to prioritize her financial well-being."

She intentionally makes time to prioritize money.

"Bonnie knows she's a goddess at managing money."

She's just as good with her own money at home as she is with the money at the office. Every financial decision aligns with her specific long-term goals and values.

"Bonnie is incredibly intelligent. She's really something."

She closely monitors financial trends and seizes financial opportunities to invest.

Her net worth has grown faster than it ever has.

The Power of Yet

It takes persistence to break a habit of negative self-talk. It's an ongoing process of noticing your self-talk, and then questioning what you hear.

For example, if you find yourself saying, "I'm such an idiot with money," your first step is to *just* notice.

"There it is again."

Don't make it worse by shaming yourself about your negative self-talk. Just observe it.

The next step is to extract the story. Most people have a few repeating stories they tell themselves about money. You have important clues about yours from your moneyisms and the flashpoints we discussed in chapter 2.

In this example, it might be true that this person has a repeating story that she's not smart enough to think about money. She may make related claims about how "Numbers make me dizzy," or "It's better for other people to take care of the money." As you identify a repeating story in your own mind, ask yourself: "Is this 100% true all the time, under every circumstance?"

If not, allow yourself to tell a new story of "yet," instead.

Carol Dweck, the theorist behind the growth mindset, calls this strategy, "The Power of Yet," in her popular TEDx talk. She describes this as a way to shift the focus away from our deficits, and instead, tap into the empowering and engaging world of what's possible. This isn't something that happens overnight. In fact, you will likely still be catching occasional instances of harsh self-talk many years into the future, especially as you stretch into bigger and bigger goals. And yet, the work you do to change the way you talk to yourself will ease a lot of stress and worry right away, long before your self-talk is in any way perfect.

Creating a list of those "yet" alternatives to your most commonly repeating stories and then using them to retrain your brain can help you replace your negative self-talk. Bringing it back to Dr. Ethan Kross, it helps to make these alternative statements in the third person.

For example, when you hear yourself say, "I'm such an idiot with my money," you will stop and notice (no shame), and then choose to reinforce this statement instead: "Maggie hasn't quite figured out how best to pay down her credit card debt, yet. But she's working on it, and she's getting much better. I'm proud of her."

Once you know what you're saying to yourself, you can decide whether or not that works for you. Next, it's time to let go of the baggage for once and for all, and then seek the support of other people.

Money Self-Talk Exercises

Harnessing your self-talk is one of the most effective ways to start changing your life for the better. Start by observing your self-talk. Our goal is to create a home base where you feel supported, comfortable, and understood. That home base needs to be in your own brain, so any self-talk that creates stress must be edited with surgery-like precision.

Write down at least three money-related thoughts and phrases you observe yourself thinking or saying. The simplest way may be to catch the thoughts in ordinary, everyday moments like each and every time you open your wallet (spend), open a statement (past spending), have a money decision to make (health insurance/benefits enrollment), are asked for money (kids, charity, etc.), or make an investment (stocks/bonds, enrolls in a course) and pay attention to what you hear.

Write or choose a baller, badass 1st person statement. For example:

- I am good with money.
- I make smart financial decisions.
- I am up-leveling my money game.

Write or choose a baller, badass 3rd person statement. For example:

- She's a badass with money.
- She has money in the bank.
- She's a money maven.

1. Can you recall a recent instance when you trash talked yourself about money? What did you say or feel? How did this self-talk impact your financial choices?

2. Reflect on a situation where you aced a financial challenge or made a wise financial decision. What positive self-talk kept you going? How did it help you succeed?

3. Envision this: you're sitting across from someone you deeply trust, a steaming cup of something comforting in your hands, and you're about to dive into the hush-hush subject of money. Imagine it. How does this conversation sound? Is it a world away from your normal chatter about dollars and cents, or is it strikingly similar?

4. Ask yourself, what bridges could you build between the money conversations you have in your own head and the ones you express out loud to your trusted confidants? Is it a matter of asking more questions, dishing out fewer judgments, or maybe just letting yourself be a bit vulnerable?

10

Connect the Dots to Your New Moneyself

*T*here's no one size fits all game plan when it comes to up-leveling your money. Directionally, it starts with the willingness to do self-exploration, and gain self-knowledge. From there, we mine the gold and connect the dots.

In the previous chapters, we've explored your past stories—your emotional financial forensics—we've identified self-talk, and written off old beliefs we're ready to move on from.

Now what we need to do is to connect the dots to what is happening in the current day and, where possible, trace present issues back to the past so we can correct old ideas and outdated beliefs. I say "where possible" because sometimes we have no recollection of why we feel what we feel about something. So we go where the pain and the debt or savings leads us and play detective.

In doing so, we expose truths about a habit's origin, falsehoods that we didn't realize we hold, beliefs that don't add up, and habits that don't support our present-day goals. Tracing the past and going to the root of it all is the fastest, easiest way to de-bunk anything that we don't really believe anyway, and re-write the beliefs and habits to align with our current values and desires, and ultimately, to get you better outcomes.

Most often, I see the potential for correctable patterns when I can talk in person with a client and identify a current pain point that they likely don't understand. This pain point in dealing with money may involve a flashback to a childhood financial flashpoint, as you learned about in chapter 2. My client Lisa demonstrated a correctable pattern in chapter 6, where she had confounded the idea that asking for a raise was like asking for a handout. Once she recognized the irrational linking of the two, she was liberated and moved up in her salary and her career.

The way to get there is to ask this question, "When in the past have you felt this way?"

It's not always beliefs that need changing—sometimes it's a flashback that needs to be traced to its root so that the presenting problem can be reframed.

Embrace Insatiable Curiosity

Money is relational. Meaning, it's most often connected to other things. If I'm being honest, it's also about being insanely curious. I'm insanely curious by nature. In the moment of witnessing a client's pain, I will ask the person every damn thing I can think of until I've exhausted my questions or I've exhausted the person.

Really, it's me trying to understand who the person is in relation to their problem. What do they think their problem is? How do they think and feel about their issue? It's probing their decision making processes to get to a full understanding.

Maybe, in a way, it's a continued search for a deeper level of understanding of why my own parents did what they did. But now I apply it to people who actually want help. I find it deeply gratifying to crack the code. And as you understand my moneyhood, the secret I kept for so long and why, my moneyself, and my anti-goal—to not live a financially erratic and insecure life, like my parents—perhaps you can see how my dots connect.

And that's not to say you do it once or five times or ten times and it's done.

It's not. This is a lifelong practice. You will continue connecting dots, mining self-knowledge, and building money skills. There will be less to do over time, but the investment you make in cracking your financial forensics and increasing your self-knowledge will pay off for every year you are alive, both emotionally and financially.

Flashbacks to Flashpoints

As we explore further, it's important to remember that not everyone is able to access—or get to—their subconscious scripts. Modern day money scripts are not the whole story. What we're really trying to get to is unresolved stuff—the stuff that causes discomfort, a bad feeling, or worse, freezing or shutting down.

Beliefs only make up half the connection. The other half is the connection between a flashback—a painful reaction or emotional response you have today—and a flashpoint. Either one or the other can pull at you. Sometimes, when a preset situation mirrors an old one, it can stir up pain or leave you feeling stuck and unsure about what to do next.

This may be best relayed in a story format, so here is an example in my own life of where I felt anxiety in a financial situation, and I traced it back, connected the dots, and did what I'm advising you to do on these pages.

Big Sweaty Carl

A vehicle is an important asset for every parent and every family, especially when there is the consideration of gear. When my first son was a baby, a coupe was a natural fit for us. As we became a family of four with two hockey and lacrosse players, we needed a roomier vehicle for all of our gear in road trips to and from hockey and lacrosse tournaments. The "SUV era" began.

Then, with the first kiddo off to college, the second not far after, and an $8,000 auto repair hanging in the balance, I was at a new life stage—one where I could bring back some magic and nostalgia in the form of a refined, sporty, and sexy little convertible.

Yee-haw—I was excited. No money vigilant tendencies holding me back—I was ready for go-time. I loved and was loyal to my car brand and I was all in on my new ride. I had pined for it, remembering a girlfriend's mother driving one in my childhood neighborhood. I drooled every time I rode my bike past their house and saw it in their driveway.

It wasn't pre-loved. It wasn't a car I picked off of the lot. I selected every bell and whistle (white with buttery brown leather interior), and placed the order myself. It was so fun to buy exactly what I wanted, zero compromise, and I loved the feeling of anticipating its arrival.

I knew when it was on the assembly line, when it had made it onto the shipping container, when it arrived at port in Rhode Island and when it was en route to the dealership. After six months of waiting, I was counting down the days. Squeeeeee! I was excited. It wasn't an outlandish purchase. Rather, I had done my inner work, and knew how to treat myself well. The purchase was right for me at this time.

The only problem was, when I called to re-confirm the delivery date, the sales manager, "Big Sweaty Carl," suddenly demanded I pay $3,120 more. It was during the pandemic, production was slower, there were fewer new models available, I don't even know. None of it made sense because we already had a signed deal. A. Signed. Deal.

Big Sweaty Carl was aggressive and intense—his hostility and impatience toward me was palpable. He talked over me and interrupted me as a way to try to dominate me. He was such a bully, that after hanging up the phone with him, I was so rattled, that it took me two hours to stop shaking.

I'd be embarrassed to say that I actually considered paying the $3,120 just to get rid of the pit in my stomach and never have to deal with him. I "would be," but I know that this happens to all of us, and I know that if we talk it out, we can do better, and do right by ourselves. Because paying that $3,120 wasn't right, and it was likely to give me a different pit in my stomach.

My completely visceral reaction to Big Sweaty Carl guy was as much about my value for justice in the car dealership as it was about a previous incident. I knew the key question to ask myself. It's "When have I felt this before?"

After some time passed, I was able to calm my nerves, walk it off, and summon my rational brain.

Third grade. Kickball field. The field was available on a first-come, first-served basis and my friends and I got there first during one lunch recess. Little Carl arrived and tried bullying us off the field. Nuh-uh. I wasn't having it. We got there first, fair and square. Besides, our game was already in progress.

When we refused to leave, Little Carl became so incensed, that he close-fist punched me in the face!

To make matters worse, our homeroom teacher gave *me* a detention too. She justified my punishment by saying "because you were involved." To me, the real reason was because she didn't think my standing up for myself was very ladylike. And, maybe my behavior wasn't, because when Little Carl got in my face, I kept my feet firmly planted in the orange dirt on the field and yelled right back.

Big Carl never physically assaulted me at the car dealership. But our conversation sure felt like a visceral punch to the face. The atmosphere with Big Carl was so intense I had to fight the urge to give into his demands because I wanted to be rid of him. After all, I might get the equivalent of being punished for being unladylike and have my car taken away.

Despite the adrenaline that made my body shake like a leaf, I faked being calm, held firm on the deal, acted shocked when Big Sweaty Carl threatened not to sell me the car, and just let him know my expectations were for him to make good on our deal. And, boom, all of this (and that I already knew how to take a punch) worked. Within days, we moved forward on the original price and the car was mine.

Learning and relearning how to maintain my sense of self while under stress, especially during conflicts, has been a lifelong practice. It's what helps me feel fear and advocate for myself anyway and what has made me become fiercely unmessable with, especially when right from wrong and my money are concerned!

Connect the Dots

Once I recognized that Little Carl from the kickball field and Big Sweaty Carl, the sales manager, were the same persona, I wanted to say, "You're who little Carl grew up to be, the bully on the car showroom floor."

I wanted to cave in, pay him what he wanted, and to get off of the phone. In some ways, it felt like a physical assault. In reality, I was feeling the emotional intensity because of the same feelings I felt on the third grade kickball field. I was projecting the same feelings of injustice—a deal is a deal—onto the car negotiation, and it took brute effort to let that go.

Connecting the dots can help us train to recognize that what we are experiencing in the present, we have also experienced in the past, often from a visceral perspective. Once we're able to recognize, "I have felt these feelings before," our rational brain can come in and say, OK, even though this feels like third grade on the kickball field, this is *not* that.

The integrity of the issue burned to my core. At the dealership, I had a signed contract. In third grade, we had a spoken contract. You don't get to change after the fact. That's the emotional similarity. Nothing else was similar. The guy was rude but not physically threatening me. He was on the phone. The beauty of this process is that it allows us to self-validate. Carl at the car dealership would never do that.

Once I was able to see the intellectual connection, I could acknowledge I was feeling the same way—so emotionally uncomfortable that I wanted to run and be done with this guy, even though it would have cost me an extra $3k. I just want to get rid of this feeling—it's so intense. Then my rational brain said, "Don't do that"—and allowed me to not give in.

It wasn't until after I got home that I realized why I was feeling so triggered and what it was tied to.

I had a signed purchase order. A friend in the car business verified that it would stand. He "listened me off the ledge." And I sure was on one—irrationally fearful the car would be sold out from under me or held for ransom if I didn't pay up. The resolution was recognizing that my thinking was irrational, and knowing to reach out for information and advice. Of course, it was super helpful to have somebody in the know.

My job then was going back and facing Big Carl and saying, "I've acted in good faith. I expect you to act in good faith. Let's stick to the deal we agreed to." And he did.

On pickup day, I had to have an unexpected conversation with myself. The entire experience was so awful I worried that it might overshadow and ruin the enjoyment of owning and driving the car. Like there might be some Big Sweaty Carl bad karma following me around.

Hell to the no.

I turned that thinking around right quickly by choosing to feel victorious.

I am a grown-ass woman. I have been through the ringer on shit like this. I perform financial miracles and literally transform people's lives emotionally and financially in their money matters for a living, and I still have this conflict.

So, dear friend, I'm standing here today to say there's no way you don't too. There's just not.

It's not about statistics and numbers. It's about how you feel. How do you feel about your money? Are you good with it? One hundred percent of the time?

Me, neither. Let's keep working to connect those dots,

and let's keep growing and evolving together. Okay? Yes, it would be awesome if we could wipe out self-sabotage entirely. Is that realistic? I don't really know. But let's make it our business to improve it dramatically, shall we?

What we need to do is ask, "When else have I felt this way?" We need to be willing to sit with the uncomfortable to get to the root answer. That's the work—that is the possibility for changing the current interaction and fast forwarding in future situations.

Connect the Dots Exercises

Déjà vu means "already seen" in French. It's that eerie sense of reliving a moment, even though one knows it's their first time encountering it. This phenomenon is often described as a fleeting and mysterious feeling of familiarity in a new or unfamiliar context. The exact cause of déjà vu remains a topic of debate among psychologists and neuroscientists, but it's believed to be related to processes within the brain that deal with memory and recognition. Next, we will explore how moments from the past might influence your current money decisions.

Have you ever experienced *financial déjà vu*, where today's feelings oddly mirror a distant past? Using the prompts below, write a detailed description of the current or recent past financial situation, noting what feels familiar or connected between past and present.

- Can you think of a financial or non-financial situation that felt familiar to you?
- The feelings, the visceral response?
- Reflect on the beliefs or values that shaped your experience. How might those same convictions have shaped your emotions?
- Think about your emotional reactions to previous challenges. Are there similarities in how you're responding now, even in a different context?
- Recall past financial flashpoints. How do they compare to the triggers in your current situation? Do you notice any patterns in your response in the present that relate to the past?

How might déjà vu awareness guide your future financial decisions?

11

Write the Eulogy

"Whether we have a little or a lot, our relationship with money can make us feel like Beverly Hillbillies at a yacht club. And I should know."

—Michelle Arpin Begina

*D*efining what it means to "talk about money" is different for everyone. Giving yourself permission to be rich (yes, queen!) or to negotiate for a raise might be examples of this. Other examples might include discussing problematic credit card spending, getting straight answers to vexing financial problems, connecting the dots from past experiences to present day, sharing a never-before-spoken secret, or a million other things.

For me, talking about money meant distinguishing between the things that my parents did with their money, shrouded in secrecy, and the impact that their poor financial choices had on me. After 30 years of silence and shame, I debated, in my mind, whether the one story I'd never told a living soul was even mine to tell: the financial fiasco where my parents blew my college fund on a yacht.

I worried it might be too personal or disloyal to let anyone outside of my family know it. After many restless nights, I finally came to the conclusion that anything that happened to me belonged to me; that my experiences were mine to tell if I chose to.

Despite the fact that I not only talked with people about their money for a living, and guided them on their paths to wealth, my professional focus never translated to my being able to talk openly about *my feelings* about *my* money. And while I was good with money, even vigilant and living a good life, I wasn't living my best life. And while I was doing well, I wasn't realizing my full financial potential—yet.

Researchers from a group called Non-Fiction found that when it comes to talking about money, people prefer to share financial "optics" over feelings and real numbers. It's easy to talk about things that reflect a fun lifestyle or are otherwise visible to other people, such as big purchases, how much our houses are worth, or vacation pictures.

It's hard to talk about the things that *really* matter, like what keeps us up at night and why, our relationship with money, past mistakes, or things we don't understand like the markets, how interest works, or our feelings. Just thinking these things, let alone talking openly, may make us feel embarrassed, remorseful, inferior, or even incompetent.

And yet, it's talking about our feelings about money and the actual numbers that are the crucial conversations. Status signaling about big ticket purchases or stock market chatter is shallow, small talk. What really counts, pardon the pun, is to make the fine print the large print by talking about things like: our gaps in knowledge, our financial concerns and questions, money relationships with yourself and others, what you think about when you think about money, your dreams, behaviors, mistakes, regrets, fears, and of course, the actual money—what you make, keep, and invest.

It was changing my mind that *money is not* private and opening my mouth to talk about it that completely changed my life. It's often the case that talking about money is what opens things up for people.

The most cathartic money conversation of my life, so far, happened when I shared the truth about my college finances—that's right, sharing the story of the yacht debacle is what changed my life. Move over silent yoga retreat, hand me a microphone. In 2019, I signed up for a public speaking class to brush up on my skills. Shortly after enrolling, a voice inside started whispering, "It's time to tell your story." I knew which story the voice meant and was not jumping for joy to tell it. To tell my story meant that I was first going to have to change my mind and make it okay to talk about money. No gracias, I was fine.

But the voice kept nudging me, "It's time to tell your story." Slowly the idea took hold. I wasn't sure that there'd be a chance to share it during my course, but wrote a few lines down just in case and promised myself I would if there was an opportunity. And because the Universe had my back, at the very end of the day, we all were asked to deliver a two minute talk about any story from our lives that we wanted. Everyone else used their time to talk about light topics like puppies and sandwiches whereas I was about to deliver a bombshell of vulnerability.

With a bad case of stage fright (racing pulse, pounding heart, nearly irresistible urge to flee), I barely kept it together as I walked the audience through the humiliation of the yacht debacle. Speaking the words out loud made me realize that I'd never allowed myself to process my trauma or to grieve over the shame and betrayal I had felt.

With the emotional liberation I experienced, I realized that I hadn't told a story at all. I had delivered **a long overdue eulogy** for the part of me that had died on the marina dock. See, for decades I lived under the shit storm of shame, believing that if my parents didn't think I was worth investing in (yanking my college fund to buy a yacht), then I must not be worth very much. Talking about money helped me to know an inner peace I never knew existed or that I even needed and that healed my soul in a way that success or money never would. No more withholding the tender parts of me from friends and loved ones. No more shame or self-sabotage. No more feelings of unworthiness and

No.

More.

Secrets.

The quality of my life has increased exponentially because my self-worth has increased. I don't hide my imperfections as much anymore because I accept myself for who and what I am. And, although there was nothing that I could say about money growing up, I've succeeded in creating the opposite experience for my sons. They know that there's nothing that they *cannot* say about it.

Healing Money Relationships

Once I finally let the cat out of the bag, I began seeing my parents' decisions through their eyes. They're flawesome humans like the rest of us. I stopped waiting for them to magically transform and show up as my fantasy parents. To them I say, "Thank you from the bottom of my piggy bank." They sure rocked my boat, but I got to learn early on who I could count on, and that the smart bet is always on me. No matter how hard or impossible it felt at the time, things always worked out when I bet on myself. I have a strong feeling that the same thing is true for you, too.

Over time, and by doing the work, the anger and resentment toward them faded away and was replaced with compassion and forgiveness. Until I changed my mind that money *is not* private, my secrets had kept me from living my best life.

I finally came to terms with the feelings of having been stunned into silence as a five-year old trying to protect her father, asked to be silent about the car purchased against my mother's wishes, and eventually silencing myself out of shame when my parents chose a yacht over my future. These realizations led to the emotional processing that allowed me to get a better handle on my emotional drivers, allowing me to better enjoy my existing abundance and reach my financial potential.

I'm not saying it was easy. Breaking up with *that* resistance and becoming able to talk about these difficult feelings about money was hard work—like a cross between an FBI hostage negotiation and a 12-step program. But so worth it, because it meant coming to terms with this early shame and betrayal—two of the key things that lead to financial self-sabotage. Those feelings had a huge impact— they froze my parents and our relationship in time, and trapped my own growth as a person. To think, all of the trauma and anguish that my parents caused could have been prevented had they simply told me the truth: that they'd changed their minds about paying for college. Money silence like this happens *all the time!* We project a lot of unresolved feelings onto money, like grief and stress, and it takes some real work to let that go.

It's often the case that talking about money and all the feelings underneath of money is what breaks things wide open. It's what closes the psychological distance between who you know that you are and who you know that you are capable of being when it comes to your money.

You can close that gap by telling the one money story you've never told anyone before—even if it's only to yourself. When you do, all the inner peace, confidence, hope, transformation, and possibility you could ever dream of are waiting for you on the other side.

Write your money eulogy.

Of your big and small disappointments. Of your trauma. Of your dream that didn't set sail the way you wanted. Of your past. Of your fantasy parents showing up. You don't have to speak it out loud—but you could. Write it like no one will ever read it.

Don't try to protect the people who loved you but failed you miserably, including yourself. Tell your truth. This is not the place to half-ass it with vague and obscure fractals of your story. Unleash the veracity of old hurts. Let them out in the sunshine. Name names. Tell truths. Validate your feelings by allowing them on the page. In order for the old bullshit to fertilize your path forward, you have to shovel it out of your past and into the light. That is how you write a money eulogy that means something.

You may not even realize you're stuck in unprocessed grief. High growth mindset people can achieve post traumatic growth without ever stopping long enough to grieve their trauma. We're busy. We cope. Do the best we can. Sometimes, we tamp and tamp and tamp it all down to the point that we're buried under the rubble of our experiences.

There is no one way to write your money eulogy. You do anything that feels good, natural, or right for you. The thing to focus on is processing and grieving any harm that was done to us and harm we caused ourselves.

The exercises below will help you process and say goodbye to some of your most painful memories. Here, we want to honor the loss and reflect on any lessons we'll take forward. When you've completed these exercises, we can start to break new ground financially. The next chapter talks about speaking up when money gets tense.

Money Eulogy Exercises

Grief is part of the process in all the things we heal. Below, I will guide you with exercises to heal your financial wounds on a deeper level than ever before. If something really heavy comes up for you, allow yourself to take whatever time you need to process your grief.

- Write a eulogy for your financial past. The dreams that slipped through your fingers, the missed chances, the wounds you've been nursing, and yes, even the good times.

Take a breath, and let your pen embrace the highs and the lows, and every tear and chuckle in between. Give words to the secrets you've whispered only to yourself. Feel the weight and the release as you jot them down.

1. Now, look back and reflect. What wisdom has your past bestowed upon you? Any regrets staring back at you, nudging you to dig deeper, understand better? Even the financial plots twists have their lessons, and sometimes, those lessons are the ones you end up thanking from the bottom of your piggy bank. I have!
2. Deliver this eulogy however your heart tells you to. Want to shout it from a mountaintop or whisper it to the wind? Go ahead. Feel like burning it as a symbol of releasing it from this life? Be my guest. Maybe just tuck it into a drawer as a little tombstone to your evolving self. Plant something alive to symbolize both an ending and a rebirth, or light a candle to illuminate your new path.

The point is, this eulogy is your own sacred space to say goodbye, make peace, and step into what comes next. So you do you. I promise, it's like setting down a burden you didn't know you were carrying.

12

Talk it Out: Validation, Information, & Advice

*N*ow that you've excavated past beliefs and habits, gained insight on your self-talk in a respectful way, acknowledged what's dead to you with the eulogy, and are connecting the dots in a meaningful way, and as you continue to work on commanding a better relationship with money, it's time you look outward and identify the conversation(s) you need to have with others to continue moving toward your full financial potential.

Many of the most well-regarded books by well-known doctors and thought-leaders acknowledge the power of being seen, heard, and validated in the healing process. This includes works such as *What Happened to You?: Conversations on Trauma, Resilience and Healing* by Dr. Brue D. Perry and Oprah Winfrey and *The Body Keeps the Score*, by Bessel A. van der Kolk, as just two examples.

In healing your money story and improving your financial trajectory, the next thing I advise is, simply put: to talk it out with someone you trust. This is to say, to seek out a person who can help you understand your situation more deeply, whether by being a sounding board, providing an outside perspective, or by giving you information and advice. Some financial advisors play all of these roles for clients, but as long as the person has your best interest at heart and, if advice is sought, is knowledgeable about your concern, you can get this kind of support from lots of people.

Overstanding

The act of hearing our own voice, out loud, instead of the one inside our head, is healing. My experience as a financial advisor is that when a client is worked up and upset about their finances, the first thing they need is to simply be heard. It's been my experience that people aren't actually talked off of ledges (financial or otherwise), they are *listened* off of ledges. The most profound sort of listening is what I call being overstood. While understanding is about the listener making sense of your story and coming to agree with some part of it, overstanding is when someone comes to know your story, where it comes from, and *how your story makes sense to you.*

Sometimes, what we need is to experience the healing impact of someone holding our hands, looking deep into our eyes, and saying, "Just tell me." If you are seeking emotional support, choose someone for whom you can do no wrong or pick someone whose opinion matters greatly. Or share your story publicly, write a letter and read it out loud and burn it—you do you. What is important is to receive respect, unconditional positive regard, acceptance, or even love, no matter what you share.

Being heard, and especially, overstood, has a profound effect on your personal financial trajectory and therefore, on the ability to reach your full financial potential. This is because experiencing overstanding quells fear and anxiety, and helps us make mental and emotional space for what is possible. It gives us the tone and the room to know the present will be solved and a better future awaits.

Take a Breather

Our brains are lazy. This isn't a criticism, but rather a biological fact. Innately, we register two types of cognitive decisions: instinctive decisions, which we make fast, and equate with survival, and analytical decisions, which require conscious, deliberate effort and affect the long term. Human beings use one of two cognitive systems, depending on the scenario.

We rely on instinctive decisions when there is a perceived or real time crunch. Think about our ancestors deciding whether a rustle in the grass means they need to hide, run, or grab a spear and kill their next meal. The cost of making the wrong decision comes quickly, as does the benefit of making the right decision.

The trouble comes when we use instinctive thinking for issues where there's an actual time delay or financial or psychological distance between the decision and the outcome. Where costs and benefits are delayed, analytical thinking is the star, producing better results. It's a slower, more thoughtful process that dives into the nitty-gritty of complex decisions. It's vital to take a breather and slow down our thinking to make financially aligned choices.

How can we slow down enough to achieve analytical thinking when we're thrust into survival, instinctive think-ing? You can start by saying two simple words to yourself. "Let's pause." Hint: it works even better if you practice those words in your calm voice. "Let's pause." You can even add to it some reassuring statements about what's not going to happen, such as, "Let's pause. We don't need to give up our gorgeous dress or smoking hot shoes, or even eat a bag of double chocolate Milanos, although we can have a couple if it'll really make us feel better. Let's pause. We've gotten this far and done well with our finances, and we will find a solution for this, too. Let's just pause."

Do you see how you can use self-talk such as this to create a loop of calm and reassurance and even keep yourself on point to pause and access your longer term thinking? You've got this if you say so—so say so.

Denise

In December of 2015, Denise experienced a series of unfortunate events in close succession: her mom died, her son was diagnosed with a mental illness, and her husband lost his job. In January, 2016, financial headlines read, "U.S. Stocks Post Worst 10-Day Start to a Year in History" and other similarly scary sentiments. Denise called me in a panic in mid-January.

As soon as I picked up the phone, she didn't even say, "Hello." She simply launched into her spiel, "I don't care what you say. Get me out of the market. I'm going to all cash." At first, I listened without responding and Denise kept talking.

She started telling me about her concerns in vague terms. I let her go on, then I asked, "What are you listening to (i.e., news sources)? What are you reading? What exactly are you hearing? Who are you hearing it from (i.e., friends, co-workers, social media)?" I listened carefully to her answers before asking more questions: "How is all of this making you feel? What thoughts and emotions are coming up for you? What is it making you worry about in particular (i.e., let's get down to the real fear)?"

After listening some more, I said, "Going to cash is an

option. I'm just wondering if there are other things you are considering doing, e.g., you could take half of your money out of the market. What are the options?"

When Denise called me, she was in her "fight or flight" instinct. When this happens, our brain is hijacked and wants to take action—almost any action—as long as it's immediate. But, the action you decide on in this messy moment of feelings and mixed-up emotions is not likely to be the action that will actually satisfy you in the long run.

This explains why Denise wanted to yank all of her money from the market and had I done that for her—no questions asked—she might have felt less anxious at the moment. However, I knew that what she *really* wanted at that moment was to feel financially secure.

Yet, her fear was preventing her from seeing what I could see. I was thinking about the Denise I know—the Denise who defines wealth as having enough to take care of her mentally ill son and extra to give back to charities supporting others diagnosed with the same mental illness. I was thinking about the one who wants to do meaningful work and be financially secure not just in this moment of market volatility, but as long as she lives.

But I knew that if I tried to talk her out of her fear, it would backfire. Instead, I had to find another action Denise could take that would also alleviate the fear and that action had to be her idea. I told Denise (a white lie) we would take whatever action she wanted including pulling all of her money out of the market. I could almost feel her muscles relax through the phone. I simply suggested we both sleep on it, digest the conversation, regroup, and have another call the next morning to get the game plan ready.

Denise agreed to my request. The next morning with a cooler head, she called and told me what she wanted to do. She asked me to start tracking her account and sending her the balances every day. Ultimately, she decided to keep her money in the market. In short, "Listening off the Ledge" made Denise feel heard and gave her the space to pause and recalibrate her decision.

Although we didn't know it at the time, this was a decisive moment for Denise. When she panic-dialed me and said, "Get me out of the market," Denise's portfolio was down $80,000 for the month of January. It's no wonder she panicked. However, had she not been able to pause, reframe the situation, and stay invested, she would have missed out on an additional $225,000 of growth in 2016. Also, a simple "back of the envelope" calculation tells me that (assuming a modest investment rate of return and given that her age at the time was 55) lost growth could have compounded into $1 million or more of lost funds over the rest of her life.

In other words, giving Denise what she needed to sleep on her first instinct resulted in potentially averting a $1 million mistake. We all live through these types of decisive moments and we have no real way of knowing the impact these decisions have on our lives in advance. This is why we need to have someone who can overstand us in these moments.

Sounding Board

We've all been there—feeling anxious, tied up, and confused about something, but we can't quite wrap our head around it. It's painful! Then, we talk it out to someone who doesn't say *anything*, and suddenly, everything makes a little more sense. It's the value of a sounding board.

I've watched this happen to my clients as they've clarified their own issues by talking to me. I recall a moment with a client who came into our meeting worked up. Her adult son had asked her to pay off his credit card debt so that he could "start over fresh." As a single mother, she had done her best to give her son a clean start to his adult life by paying for his college degree so he could graduate without loans, and giving him a living allowance into his mid-twenties so that he could take a lower paying job early in his career. To do these things, she had worked long hours at a demanding job, and felt guilty that she hadn't been home more for her son.

Now in his early thirties, he was asking her to pay off a large credit card debt that he had accrued by living above his means. She came into our meeting worried that she had given him too much support. Had she done enough to help him develop financial independence? After reviewing her own financial numbers, she expressed her worries to me, saying, "It would be one thing if I had the money to pay off his credit card with no problem, but I'm heading into retirement and it would be financially precarious to me to pay them off this time." I was opening my mouth to say that it sounded like she had her answer, when she said, "Well, I guess I answered my own question. I just can't. Not because I don't want to help him, but because I have to think about my own long-term financial health."

Sometimes our own words, said out loud to an empathetic ear, can serve as a flashlight through the dark tunnel of our minds. And this is before the other person has contributed anything of their own value to the conversation.

Outside Perspectives

Getting an outside perspective is an important part of learning to talk about money. When left to their own devices, our brains default to extremes, creating a tendency to think in black-and-white, all-or-nothing scenarios. Sometimes, when we are missing that outside perspective, we are likely to flip-flop between thinking that the worst will happen and denying that there's a problem at all. When this happens, it's difficult to be objective and matter-of-fact about your money concerns, as Grace demonstrated in chapter 9, as she remained worried and stuck for eight years with her tax issues and straddling the idea of a full-time job and entrepreneurship.

I see this often with entrepreneurs that I work with. Fear of not making enough money in the coming months will prompt them to start siphoning their expenses off to credit cards. This means that their expenses are even more because of the interest they pay on their credit debt which reinforces the feeling of not having enough. This is the consequence of all-or-nothing thinking, which has a tendency to reinforce itself.

When I work with clients who find themselves hiding their expenses behind their credit cards, I provide the outside perspective. It's next to impossible to get enough perspective on our own to see what's outside of our normal view. I help my clients to look at their actual numbers, so they can see that with the right plan, they have more than enough money to pay their expenses, and help them to start saving for the inevitable ups and downs of entrepreneurship. When we have someone knowledgeable giving us an outside perspective, we can rise above black and white thinking. Without this outside perspective, we're more likely to second-guess our abilities when we hit rough patches and stay stuck right where we are.

Ryan & Morgan:
Advice, Information, and Problem Solving

When I first met Ryan and Morgan, a self-employed couple, they had saved hundreds of thousands toward retirement, but were also $60,000 in debt. The truth was, they had saved too aggressively. Because their savings ate into their cash flow, they relied on credit cards to make up the difference on their monthly bills. What started with good intentions (saving for retirement), was executed without a longer-term plan, and resulted in high interest debt.

It took some time before Ryan and Morgan were ready to brainstorm solutions to pay off their debts. We spent our first six months delving into their moneyhood, discovering what had caused their debt to escalate. Even though they were making significant payments on their credit cards, they continued to use them to make purchases. No surprise, the balance stayed the same. This was when we realized that though the habit began as a means of making up for aggressive saving, it was compounded by their lack of awareness of what they were spending their money on.

Using a whiteboard in my office, we laid out all of their debts. It is often the case that looking at our actual numbers reveals a truth we can no longer ignore.

Fast-forward about nine months: Morgan and Ryan are sticking to their plan putting $5,000 per month toward their debt while changing their daily routine. Morgan, who had been working part time, has started working extra hours each week. She also stopped taking taxis as often, which saved them about $800 per month (that's NYC for you!). They temporarily reduced their travel budget—which they both love—to lower expenses. As they become more aware of their spending and earning habits, they're on track to pay off their debt ahead of schedule. I'm so proud of them.

When I asked them during our first meeting, "What

does it mean to be good with money?" they said, knowing what to do with their money. Morgan and Ryan are perfect examples of two people who learned to cultivate a wealth skill. They now know what to do with their money because they are aware of where their money is going and what they can afford. They'll be back to their full travel routine again soon.

We Can Do Hard Things

Money can be difficult to talk about for at least two reasons. First, money touches everything: almost all of our relationships, your personal and work life, and most of our hobbies and commitments. Everything either costs something, involves negotiating for resources, or taps into expectations that other people have about how money should, could, or will be spent.

Yet, in the words of Glennon Doyle, "We can do hard things."

Whether you are looking for someone to hear you out or give you critical advice, it's time to reach out and ask for help. For some people, this will be a simple matter of googling a phone number of a financial therapist or financial advisor and making the call. For others, it can be the item on the to-do list that carries from day to day for weeks, months, years.

Choose someone who you believe can provide over-standing, a sounding board, an outside perspective, or the information and advice you need to problem solve together: a friend, family member, colleague, financial therapist, or financial advisor. Choose that person, call them up, and schedule a time to talk.

If you're struggling with the concept of asking for help, please know that you are not alone. Social psychologist,

Heidi Grant, explains just how difficult it is to ask for help, arguing that our minds process social pain in much the same way we process physical pain; the same areas of our brain involved with feeling an intense muscle cramp are involved in feeling social inadequacy and embarrassment.

My advice: acknowledge the pain. Self-validate. Write a supportive and encouraging script in third person. Trust your instincts, and use the five-second rule authored by Mel Robbins; i.e., count yourself backwards 5-4-3-2-1 and make your move.

When we're in the grip of anxiety or shame, it may be hard to imagine that we have much more to gain than to lose by opening up, but we do. Calculating your next steps to find your voice means figuring out how to share your problems with others who can help. And when you do, you'll change the course of your financial future.

Break the Silence Exercises

Take a moment. Consider where you were when you picked up this book and started chapter 1, and where you are now. Look how far you've come in your understanding of financial drivers and your own self-knowledge. You understand what secrecy bias is and the havoc it can wreak. You've considered how financial flashpoints and moneyisms have impacted your life. You're shaking up both your inner belief system and your identity. Your self-talk is less jerky. You've grieved, and said your goodbyes to your financial past, and you're ready to step into a future bright with promise and possibility.

- Write down three to five new distinctions about your financial life that you have now, that you didn't before.

THIS IS YOUR LAUNCHPAD. You're prepped and ready to break the silence and have those heart-to-heart talks about money—with real, live humans. We're talking fears, dreams, flubs, and uncertainties, all put on the table, ready for you to learn, lean on others, and grow.

So, what's left? Just a few pointed questions to prime you for the real talk with a worthy conversation partner:

1. Who in your life can help you take a breather— slow your roll just enough so you can hear your own thoughts? A parent, sibling, mentor, friend, colleague? Who can overstand you?
2. Who are your financial collaborators? Co-creators?
3. Who has your best interest at heart?
4. Ask yourself, where are those knowledge gaps? Who's got the know-how, wisdom, or advice you need?
5. Craving some perspective? Who can offer that kind of intellectual balm?
6. Who has been in your shoes and wears the one that you want to be wearing?
7. What keeps you up at night?
8. Which mistakes are you done repeating?
9. Finally, who do you trust with the raw, unfiltered you—the one with all the feelings about money and its intricate tango with your life?

Now that this truth has found you, don't dillydally! Find your voice, start talking, leverage it to greater outcomes and don't *ever* stop!

13

Abracadabra!

*J*essica Knoll is the bestselling author of *Bright Young Women, The Favorite Sister,* and *Luckiest Girl Alive,* also a major motion picture released by Netflix. In her April 2018 New York Times op-ed *I Want to Be Rich and I'm Not Sorry,* she explains, "Success, for me, is synonymous with making money. I want to write books, but I really want to sell books. I want advances that make my husband gasp and fat royalty checks twice a year. I want movie studios to pay me for option rights and I want the screenwriting comp to boot." She spoke in such raw and unapologetic terms about money meaning power to her that people rushed the exits to respond online like peak demand on an electrical grid.

Within twenty-four hours of her op-ed being published, there were 1,094 comments. All of which I read (I know, get a life, Michelle!) with the same level of interest as the article itself. Every aspect of humanity—we each see in it what we want to see—was on display in the comments as a veritable "treatise on money" as described by a screen meme named Tiger Shark. Sentiments ranged between "you go, girl," and "go to hell, girl." Many held Ms. Knoll up as an example of who not to be. Others hoped their daughters would follow her example to declare their own financial independence free of other people's opinions. There were as many cheers as there was awe and pity for Jessica as there was belief that all rich people, except Bill Gates and Warren Buffet, are bad. They called Jessica angry while they themselves seemed pissed off at her audacity to want her cake and to eat it too. Some justified her desire to be rich so long as her money was used to emancipate other women by fixing the broken system that once caused her powerlessness and had also created her. In return for speaking her mind, she was unfavorably compared multiple times to a certain former, bombastic, White House occupant and held up as Muhammad Ali once was as yet another ego maniac declaring herself the greatest (writer).

Unapologetic

Jessica's story is an example of self-permission—she's unapologetic about her goal: she wants to make money. She also has a great example of anti-goals—she doesn't ever want to feel powerless again, and wants to get to the place where she has choices: live life as a writer, drive a Porsche, sell books, earn jaw-dropping sums of money, value creativity and financial independence. That she declared, "I want to be rich," in a NY Times op-ed speaks volumes that she thinks for herself and isn't being held back by who people think she is.

Jessica's true power doesn't come from money at all but from a deep and intimate knowing—despite being underes-timated and patronized by others at times—of what she was born for. It's the kind of belief in self one must have to detach from other people's opinions. It's the strength to live on purpose and claim our rewards. Her sense of purpose and worth are priceless and *more* powerful than money.

When we accept the lies of others or the ones that we tell ourselves, we shut down our way of being in the world. We don't express ourselves fully or get to know and really understand who we are so that we can build confidence and self-assurance. It's easier to conform, safer to hide, and much less likely we'll open up to talk about the shame or guilt that disconnects us from our true selves, what we desire, and what is meant for us.

The Will *Is* the Way

We've all heard the common saying, "Where there's a will, there's a way." But when push comes to shove, "will" is so much more than that. When we rise above our circumstances to a bigger version of what life can be, the will *is* the way. And the way of the will is much more dynamic than willpower alone. It takes more than willpower to reach our boldest financial ambitions: it takes self-awareness, drive, ambition, purpose, and ultimately, leaps of faith.

It's popular to attribute intelligence and self-control as the deciding factors that bring the figments of our imaginations to life. Entire books have been written about willpower with a singular focus on the need to regulate and replenish depleted stores of emotional and mental energy. Scarcely a word is devoted to the source of energy from which our will derives its power in the first place. The human act of will is a profound odyssey.

Within each of us is an intelligence that belongs to our higher consciousness and a psychological existence that holds our past, present, and our future. Who we are and who we are becoming are parts of our will that drive us toward the future that we want. The true essence of will is its ability to channel our entire being, directing us to lead a life not only of purpose but one that resonates with our deepest essence.

Our will is the wind beneath our wings, an invisible hand that infuses the ego with the soul. We are all seekers on life's journey, trying to find and express ourselves, and money is often an expression of self, or at least a tool to do so. The will isn't associated with knowledge or mindset. The will draws from the intimate connection we have with our essential self. We bring things to life by using all of the will's dimensions. We may want to do, be, or have something, yet desire alone is not enough to manifest our dream. It is through deliberate practice over time, accessing all aspects of the will—strong will, skilled will, good will, and transcendent will—that we are able to mobilize a sense of direction and forward momentum in our lives.

The most familiar and misunderstood aspect of the will is the strong will. We think being strong-willed constitutes the whole will and means to be opinionated and stubborn. But that's not the whole truth. Being of strong will is not the whole will, nor is it simply being opinionated and stubborn. It is that and the intense spark that lights you up initially and carries enough fire within you to keep you going.

Our strong will is a sacred and divine place that our true self calls home. It's how the profound knowing of the purpose of our existence and of what is right and meant for us is expressed. This place is quiet and whispers the secrets that are hidden within. It can easily be drowned out by the noise of the world that we live in. If we're not intentional about listening and leading our lives according to what we know to be true, our overactive imagination will rush in to fill the void to play roles in life which aren't meant for us. We then suffer the experience of false beliefs. These are the worst: accepting other people's bullshit about what's right for us or accepting lies that we tell ourselves as truth.

An Act of Reclamation

Developing a strong will is an act of reclaiming a world that has been lost to us, sometimes as far back as childhood. It's a journey to the center of the earth: the fantastic limitless inner world that exists within us all that brings us back to authenticity and restores inner balance and harmony.

In my case, I was dead-set on going to college, and nothing in the world was going to stop me: not my parents' betrayal, not having zero dollars, not having no plan, not even having no idea what I was doing. Nothing was going to stop me. That's will. The reclamation part was me foraging for that Plan B, doing it when I was afraid anyway, and doubling down on myself.

Opening up to family members for emotional support or asking for financial help was out of the question. They would have wanted to know details about what had happened which carried too much shame for me to open up about at the time. How I'd make a living or afford to make loan payments wasn't clear, so taking on student loans felt too risky. Getting a job seemed like a reasonable option to pursue. I figured I'd pay my way through college as I went along.

Within a few months, I had a full-time job as a teller at a small, regional bank; the timing coincided with the start of the new school year. As part of the onboarding process, the branch manager offered for me to take an introduction to banking course at the local community college. She explained the corporate benefit of tuition reimbursement, where all full-time employees that successfully completed job-related, college courses were eligible to be reimbursed the tuition costs. I was gobsmacked.

There we stood, in a dingy basement breakroom having a life-changing conversation, seemingly out of the blue, which was to become *my way forward*. What were the odds? As someone who'd been trying to find order among the mental chaos and uncertainty, I felt like this was spiritual guidance—a sign that I was on the right track.

It took me 10 years of full-time jobs and part-time classes but I did it—I got my associate's degree at community college, and then my bachelor's degree at Rider University.

Tapping into Your Strong Will

My conviction to go to college was clear and the will to make it happen was so strong that it burned inside of me. Knowing exactly what I wanted and what was meant for me was almost the only thing going for me at the time because the path forward, or waypower, was definitely not clear. This is the kind of unreasonableness and irrationality that we think of as the hallmarks of being strong-willed: the determination and single-mindedness to make a go of things in spite of the odds against us. Daniel Kahneman, the late psychologist and Nobel Prize laureate for his work on the psychology of judgment and decision-making, explained on the *WorkLife with Adam Grant podcast*, "It is clear that some people who are irrationally persistent achieve great success. Indeed, if you look back at great successes, you will generally find that there is some irrational persistence behind them and an irrational optimism …"

Tapping into your strong will is a lesson in owning your power. For me, this was an early lesson on honoring what my heart was set on and to believe that what I wanted was possible even though I could not yet see how I'd make my vision a reality. That my parents went back on their word was irrelevant and had no bearing or power to take my ambitions away from me. Getting an education was no longer something to be given or earned, it was something to be taken. Pure and simple, what moved me forward was faith, as in the Universe-had-my-back kind of faith. What else could explain knowing that things were hopeless and yet being determined to make them otherwise? Under the circumstances, trusting myself and having faith were the right uses of my imagination.

The Magic Word

I'd be lying if I told you there was one magical formula to liberate yourself from the secrecy and shame that is inherent in most people when it comes to money. There's not. Writers like Jessica Knoll and others understand the profound power of words better than most. They grasp that words educate and shape our perspectives of the world, one another, and ourselves. They go straight to our head and hold immense power over our emotional states and our inner and outer reality.

You're always going to feel alone—as if money is just a little outside of your reach—if you're not talking about it with people who know more than you, people who are creating things with you, because money only has value through the exchange of it.

Seeking financial advice from an accountant was

Grace's equivalent of making a pit stop during a long journey, where she refueled, cleaned the windshield, and asked for directions that ultimately transformed her financial life.

Lisa broke free from her misconception that requesting a raise was like asking for charity, leading to a breakthrough in her career and salary.

Once Tara let her inner Scrooge McDuck go, her perspective on achieving financial security broadened. She no longer avoids money and instead approaches it like a fact of life.

EJ rewired his brain, replacing his deep-seated belief that "Money isn't important," with "Money isn't everything, but it is important," and transformed himself from big spender to prudent financial decision-maker.

When Andrew's overspending escalated, he realized he was on the cusp of losing everything. Once he openly acknowledged the truth, he was able to make different choices and ultimately prevail over his financial self-sabotage.

Spending on the finer things in life is so much fun. I got that from my parents. Despite all financial evidence to the contrary, at times I feared I was being a spendthrift—spending my prosperity just as they had.

"Is this extravagant purchase really necessary, or am I repeating their mistakes? Should I be more frugal and save instead?"

To help me see the financial forest for the trees, I went to the source—my husband, who had the insight and personal knowledge of the truth. I shared my concerns about being a spendthrift, and he simply asked me, "Does a spendthrift have her kids' college accounts locked and loaded? Or retirement accounts that are ahead of schedule?"

His questions reassured me and allowed me to let go of my irrational fear.

My sons are remarkably candid about finances. I've often thought about turning their moneyisms into a merchandising venture—tee-shirts proclaiming, "I told those jerks no taxes from my paycheck," or "My problem. Your money."

Years from now, they won't be saying, "No one taught me about money." I've made sure of that. When they inquire, I lay it all bare—my income, investments, and even the exact date the mortgage will finally be history. And because I have, they know how to talk about money.

When my personal "Titanic" struck the iceberg, I disassociated. I remained in survival mode for the first half of my life, trying to use my intellect to break down barriers instead of addressing my deep shame and betrayal. It was only when I acted on the voice inside that said, "It's time to tell your story," that I found inner peace alongside the abundance in my life.

To get to that place, I had to really, really "go there."

To enjoy the abundance you already have and reach your full financial potential, you'll need to do the same—facing your own challenges head-on.

Trust me.

It will be worth it.

I know you can do it too.

In my mind's eye when the big day arrived, I would walk into a Bursar's office. I would slide a check across a desk to the person in charge as payment for my eldest son's first semester college tuition.

Times have changed; no one writes checks these days—everything's digital. So, when the time came, it felt anticlimactic to press a button and have the money vanish into the ether. This was too significant a moment to let pass unnoticed. Should I have ordered a cake? Or perhaps taken that epic nine-hour round trip to deliver the tuition in person? In the end, we huddled around my laptop as a family, hitting the submit button together.

No words were exchanged because I was far too choked up to speak, but we didn't need words. They had long since been spoken. We simply hugged it out in front of the screen, in a quiet moment of understanding and shared pride.

Using your voice is one of the most underestimated and overlooked parts of being good with money and the most direct way to realize your full financial potential.

Words are the most profound connection to the very essence of magic.

From my earliest memories, I thought that the word "abracadabra" was just playful gibberish magicians used to conjure rabbits from hats. Learning its true meaning was as thrilling as finding hidden treasure might be. It filled me with the same sense of astonishment and delight as watching magic tricks once did as a child.

Translated from Aramaic, abracadabra means, "What I speak is what I create."

Your words are your wand, your incantation, your "abracadabra!"

Use them.

It's your time.

Bibliography

Financial Plot Twist

Allison Fallon. *The Power of Writing It Down: A Simple Habit to Unlock Your Brain and Reimagine Your Life.* Grand Rapids, MI: Zondervan, 2021.

Secrecy Bias

Ally Financial. "Holiday Tip: Most Americans Say Social Conversations About Money are Taboo." Accessed 3/15/22. https://media.ally.com/2015-11-24-Holiday-Tip-Most-Americans-Say-Social-Conversations-About-Money-are-Taboo-According-to-Ally-Banks-Money-Talks-Study.

Michelle Arpin Begina. "Talking About Money Is Easy Once You Know How," TEDxBayonne, April 22, 2022, https://youtu.be/08rIG9SsQL0?si=BpWx097PFKhBWkvS.

Dr. Howard Farkas. Interview with the author, June 23, 2022.

FINRA. "2090. Know Your Customer." Accessed 12/8/2023. https://www.finra.org/rules-guidance/rulebooks/finra-rules/2090.

Nonfiction Research. "The Secret Financial Lives of Americans: and the Future of Financial Services." Accessed 09/15/2021. https://drive.google.com/file/d/1E6txMhzWLornjpvqDVRbDnloGfkq1fx8/view.

Pew Research Center. "Many Americans Continue to Experience Mental Health Difficulties as Pandemic Enters Second Year." March 16, 2021. Accessed 11/15/2023. https://www.pewresearch.org/fact-tank/2021/03/16/many-americans-continue-to-experience-mental-health-difficulties-as-pandemic-enters-second-year/.

Michael Slepian. *The Secret Life of Secrets: How Our Inner Worlds Shape Well-Being, Relationships, and Who We Are.* New York: Crown, 2022.

World Health Organization. "Suicide." Accessed 11.13.2023. https://www.who.int/news-room/fact-sheets/detail/suicide.

Financial Self-Sabotage & the Four Emotional Money Drivers

Dr. Howard Farkas. Interview with the author, June 23, 2022.

A. Srivastava, E. A. Locke, and K. M. Bartol. "Money and Subjective

Well-Being: It's Not the Money, It's the Motives." *Journal of Personality and Social Psychology* 80(6): 959–971. https://doi.org/10.1037/0022-3514.80.6.959.

Your Moneyhood

Judith Barr, MS, LMHC. "A Recession Regression: Finding the Root of Our Relationship with Money." https://judithbarr.com/portfolio/a-recession-regression-finding-the-root-of-our-relationships-with-money/.

A. Furnham, S. von Stumm, and R. Milner. "Moneygrams: Recalled Childhood Memories about Money and Adult Money Pathology." *Journal of Financial Therapy* 5 (1): 4. https://doi.org/10.4148/1944-9771.1059.

R. Kemnitz, B. T. Klontz, and K. L. Archuleta. "Financial Enmeshment: Untangling the Web." *Journal of Financial Therapy* 6 (2): 32–48.

Brad Klontz, Edward Horwitz, and Ted Klontz. *Money Mammoth: Harness the Power of Financial Psychology to Evolve Your Money Mindset, Avoid Extinction, and Crush Your Financial Goals.* 1st ed. Hoboken, NJ: John Wiley & Sons, 2021.

Money Scripts

Laura B. Aknin, et al. "Prosocial Spending and Well-Being: Cross-Cultural Evidence for a Psychological Universal." *Journal of Personality and Social Psychology* 104 (4): 635–652. https://doi.org/10.1037/a0031578.

Dr. Howard Farkas. Interview with the author, June 23, 2022.

B. Klontz, S. L. Britt, J. Mentzer, and T. Klontz. "Money Beliefs and Financial Behaviors: Development of the Klontz Money Script Inventory." *Journal of Financial Therapy* 2 (1): 1. https://doi.org/10.4148/jft.v2i1.451.

Britt Klontz. "How Clients' Money Scripts Predict Their Financial Behaviors." *Journal of Financial Planning* (November): 33-43.

B. Klontz, S. L. Britt, K. L. Archuleta, and T. Klontz. "Disordered Money Behaviors: Development of the Klontz Money Behavior Inventory." *Journal of Financial Therapy* 3 (1): 2. https://doi.org/10.4148/jft.v3i1.1485.

D. Lawson, B. Klontz, and S. Britt. 2015. "Money Scripts." In *Financial Therapy*, edited by B. Klontz, S. Britt, and K. Archuleta, 23-34. Cham: Springer. https://doi.org/10.1007/978-3-319-08269-1_3.

Your Moneyself

J. E. Marcia. "Development and Validation of Ego-Identity Status." *Journal of Personality and Social Psychology*, 3(5), 551.

J. E. Marcia. "Identity in Adolescence." *Handbook of Adolescent Psychology*, 9(11), 159-187.

Barbara Waxman. *The Middlescence Manifesto: Igniting the Passion of Midlife.* Kentfield, CA: The Middlescence Factor, 2016.

The Duality of Money—How to Allow What We Want

Sarah D. Asebedo. "Three Essays on Financial Self-Efficacy Beliefs and the Saving Behavior of Older Pre-Retirees." PhD dissertation, Kansas State University, 2016. https://krex.k-state.edu/bitstream/handle/2097/32734/SarahAsebedo2016.pdf

Board of Governors of the Federal Reserve System. "2022 Survey of Consumer Finances." https://www.federalreserve.gov/econres/scfindex.htm.

S. J. Huston. "Measuring Financial Literacy." *The Journal of Consumer Affairs* 44 (2): 296-316.

Daniel Kahneman and Amos Tversky. "Prospect Theory: An Analysis of Decision under Risk." *Econometrica* 47 (2): 263-291.

Nonfiction Research. "The Secret Financial Lives of Americans: and the Future of Financial Services." Accessed 9/15/02021. https://drive.google.com/file/d/1E6txMhzWLornjpvqDVRbDnlo Gfkq1fx8/view.

Command Your New Money Relationship

American Psychological Association. "2022 Stress in America Survey." https://www.apa.org/topics/stress/holiday-money.

Anandi Mani, Sendhil Mullainathan, Eldar Shafir, and Jiaying Zhao, "Poverty Impedes Cognitive Function," *Science Magazine*, August 2013, Vol. 341, Issue 6149, pp. 976-980 https://science.sciencemag.org/content/341/6149/976.

Amanda, Crowell, PhD. *Great Work: Do What Matters Most Without Sacrificing Everything Else.* Glen Ridge, NJ: Amanda Crowell Companies, 2022.

James O. Prochaska, John C. Norcross, and Carlo C. DiClemente. "Applying the stages of change." *Psychotherapy in Australia* 19, no. 2 (2013): 10-15.

Self-Talk—The Invisible Force

Ethan Kross. *Chatter: The Voice in Our Head, Why It Matters, and How to Harness It.* New York: Crown, 2021.

Carol Dweck, "The Power of Yet," TEDxNorrkoping, 9/12/2014. https://youtu.be/J-swZaKN2Ic?si=U0PSitPuMlfULbkq.

Connect the Dots to Your New Moneyself

A. M. Cleary, A. S. Brown, B. D. Sawyer, J. S. Nomi, A. C. Ajoku, & A. J. Ryals. "Familiarity from the Configuration of Objects in 3-dimensional Space and Its Relation to Déjà Vu: A Virtual Reality Investigation." *Consciousness and Cognition* 21 (2): 969–75.

H. Eichenbaum, A. P. Yonelinas, & C. Ranganath. "The Medial Temporal Lobe and Recognition Memory." *Annual Review of Neuroscience* 30: 123–52.

A. R. O'Connor & C. J. A. Moulin. "Recognition Without Identification, Erroneous Familiarity, and Déjà Vu." *Current Psychiatry Reports* 12 (3): 165–73.

C. J. A., Moulin, M.A. Conway, R. G. Thompson, N. James, & R. W. Jones. "Disordered Memory Awareness: Recollective Confabulation in Two Cases of Persistent Déjà Vecu." *Neuropsychologia* 43 (9): 1362–78.

Write the Eulogy

Nonfiction Research. "The Secret Financial Lives of Americans: and the Future of Financial Services." Accessed 9/15/2021. https://drive.google.com/file/d/1E6txMhzWLornjpvqDVRbDnloGfkq1fx8/view.

Talk it Out: Validation, Information & Advice

Heidi Grant. *Reinforcements: How to Get People to Help You.* Harvard Business Review Press, 2018.

Daniel Kahneman. *Thinking, Fast and Slow.* New York: Farrar, Straus and Giroux, 2011.

Mel Robbins. "How to Stop Screwing Yourself Over." TEDxSanFrancisco, June 11.https://www.ted.com/talks/mel_robbins_how_to_stop_screwing_yourself_over.

The Urban Dictionary. 2023. "Overstand." Accessed October 31, 2023. https://www.urbandictionary.com/define.php?term=overstand.

Abracadabra!

Roberto Assagioli. *The Act of Will*. Synthesis Center Inc., 2010.

Adam Grant. "Daniel Kahneman Doesn't Trust Your Intuition." *Work/Life with Adam Grant*, March 2021. https://www.ted.com/talk/ staken_for_granted_daniel_kahneman_doesn_t_trust_your_intuition

Jessica Knoll. "I Want to Be Rich and I'm Not Sorry." The New York Times, April 18. https://www.nytimes.com/2018/04/28/opinion/ sunday/women-want-to-be-rich.html.

Take It to The Bank (Acknowledgments)

Mom, if I had a dollar for every time you said, "It's what's inside that counts," well, you know the rest. I've taken your words to the bank, and because of you, I understand the real meaning of wealth.

Truer words were never spoken than yours, Dad, "It's not what you say, but how you say it." A truth so profound, it could only be rivaled by the silence of unspoken things. Love you, but did you *have to* pull so much crap?

My heartfelt gratitude, Denise Brosseau, for daring to ask what *the one story* I never told was. The question sowed the seed for my voice to find its expression.

Never intending to tell my story for the first time to a complete stranger, Robin Amos Kahn, your unconditional positive regard was transcendent. The day we met marks the end of "before" and the beginning of an entirely new "after."

Dr. Amanda Crowell, without your commitment to get me out of my own way, this book would still be a kitchen sink of incoherent thoughts. Your great work inspires mine!

Kristina Paider, a.k.a. Detective Lacey—book doctor extraordinaire. You rearranged the deckchairs on the lido deck, somehow giving *Be Good with Money* its backbone and structure. Keep saying yes to my crazy questions, ok?

Choi Messer, you created a book cover so beautiful it makes the words inside seem better.

Anna Paradox, your meticulous copy editing and proof-reading have been a treasure, illuminating my words with an artful mastery of language. Those lovely little notes in the margins were like finding Easter eggs in a very wordy hunt.

AJ Harper, your guidance in the Top Three Author Book Club and dedication to helping authors write impactful books significantly shaped my words. You inspire me both on and off the page.

Laura Stone—my personal Dallas Cowboys cheerleader—for reminding me a killer idea naturally gathers its crowd.

To the entire team at Book Whisperer who made his book a reality, thank you. You're the real deal.

My thanks to Dr. Howard Farkas for sharing his refreshing addition to the theory of self-sabotage with me. I am grateful for the brief yet meaningful time we spent, taken too soon from this world. I cherish the words you've left behind.

Amanda Cessor, Sam Doka, Kate Eckman, Ruth Gaviria, Susan Marzi, Adriana Mateus, Kath Ritter, Fanna Sharma, D'Arcy Webb and Mara Yale—you all provided early reader feedback with the precision of a Swiss watch. Thank you for sharing a passion to bring the best possible work into the world.

Megan McNealy, your encouragement and shimmery light always spills over, helping me shine more brightly, a reflection of your own luminous spirit.

Susan Eckstein, your courage to live your truth is a testament to the power of authenticity. Our many "talk out loud" conversations fostered a deeper understanding and clarity of thought, enriching both my ideas and our bond.

Michelle Kaplan, reinventing while brilliantly maintaining your essence, you demonstrate the art of transformation while staying true to one's core. Thank you for leading the way.

For my husband Mike, your unwavering faith played a quiet, yet vital role in boosting my resolve to complete this book. You are my rock.

Alex and Nick, you've patiently waited and watched, wise beyond your years, as your mother stumbled her way to authorship. This journey, with its endless drafts, moments of self-doubt and joy, wasn't just about writing a book; it was a pilgrimage to the heart of *who we are*. In following our true callings, we don't just do something; we become catalysts for a better world, and if we're really lucky, we also move closer to realizing our full potential.

About the Author

Michelle Arpin Begina is on a mission to teach people how to talk about money. As a senior financial advisor and changemaker, she brings wisdom and guts to money conversations. While not the first to work her way through college, Michelle did so against an unheard of backdrop of family betrayal and financial secrets. She is an Investopedia 100 Top Financial Advisor, TEDx speaker, and successfully lobbied for K-12 financial psychology education in her home state of New Jersey. Connect with her at michelleab.com or on social media:

facebook.com/michelle.arpinbegina

instagram.com/themichelleab

linkedin.com/in/michellearpinbeginacfp

substack.com/@michelleab